Buttercup j

Buttercup Jill

PEGGY GRAYSON

Farming Press

First published 1994

A catalogue record for this book is available from
the British Library

ISBN 0-85236 270 6

*Published by Farming Press Books, Wharfedale Road,
Ipswich IP1 4LG, United Kingdom*

Distributed in North America
by Diamond Farm Enterprises,
Box 537, Alexandria Bay, NY 13607, USA

Cover design by Andrew Thistlethwaite

The illustration on the front cover is reproduced from a
poster entitled 'Join the Women's Land Army'. It was
originally issued by the Ministry of Labour and National
Service in conjunction with the Ministry of Agriculture.

Typeset by Galleon Typesetting
Printed and bound in Great Britain by Biddles Ltd,
Guildford and King's Lynn

CONTENTS

PREFACE

For I can plough and milk a cow
And I can reap and mow,
I'm as fresh as the daisy as grows in the field,
And they calls I Buttercup Joe.

OLD ENGLISH COUNTRY BALLAD

There it was, hanging on the wall of the museum, a three-legged milking stool, and underneath a plate which read: 'Milking stool used in primitive farming in olden times.' Primitive? Olden? Ye gods, I spent much of my early life perched on one of these 'primitive' items—am I that old?

From a very small child I longed to be a farmer, to the dismay of my mother who wondered why the only child of her second marriage should turn out to be such a tomboy. My early exploits on farms prepared me for the real thing: the Women's Land Army. I dearly longed to be 'Buttercup Joe,' but was happy to settle for 'Buttercup Jill.'

CHAPTER ONE

Uncle Henry took to his bed on his seventieth birthday and announced that he intended to stay there till he died. He was a very determined old gentleman and carried out his threat, remaining recumbent for nearly five years until he was conveyed to his final resting place.

Uncle Henry was a farmer, working a small acreage in what was, in the mid 1920s, darkest Gloucestershire, with the assistance of his daughter, Cousin Rene, and an occasional helping hand at hay, harvest and muck spreading. When Uncle Henry took to his bed it was in the middle of a fine May day, and he went under the sheets, fully dressed and with his socks on, and refused to remove any of his garments saying they would 'see him out.' In vain did his desperate daughter beg him to disrobe; friends came in to add their voices, but they, and even the District Nurse, failed. The latter, a formidable dragon on a sit-up-and-beg bicycle, washed her hands of him completely, declaring he was an old fraud, there was nothing wrong with him and the sooner he got up and back to work the better. She even left without the obligatory cup of tea, slamming the back door so loudly that a jug jumped off a hook on the dresser and smashed on the stone floor. This state of affairs continued for nearly two months, and when all entreaties failed and the stench became overpowering throughout the house, Cousin Rene sent for my father.

My father was one of four brothers of a notable Bristol milling family. The eldest brother, Uncle Ernest, died in middle age from sleeping sickness contracted from a boat in the docks whence he went to check a cargo of some substance for the family business. His parents, heartbroken at the early demise of their favourite son, followed him in the same year. I never knew my paternal grandparents: they refused to meet my mother as she had been divorced and so they considered her a scarlet woman; the fact that my father had also been divorced never occurred to them.

The second brother was Uncle Jim, christened Graham, who had served some years in the Royal Navy. He was a jolly man, kept afloat by a bottle of Johnny Walker a day. Then came my father, who had been put, against his will it was said, into the Army; he also found that a sustaining beverage helped him to forget the rigours of the South African War and the horrors of the 1914 conflict. The fourth brother was Uncle Ted whose greatest claim to fame seemed to be the siring of six children.

When there was a crisis it was my father, incredibly impecunious and unstable but with a heart of gold, a silver tongue and the ability to get anyone out of a jam except himself, for whom the family sent. When Uncle Ernest died it was my father who had to make the family visits to his poor widow who was incarcerated in a lunatic asylum, despite the fact that anyone a bit short of a full load terrified him. So, it was only natural that when Uncle Henry, grandfather's younger brother, became too unsanitary to live with, Cousin Rene sent for my father.

Daddy's description of the visit kept him in pints and dinners for quite some time, as he was a superb raconteur with a lively imagination. One never really knew where truth started and imagination took over; whichever, it made for hilarious listening.

Daddy arrived at the farm late one evening in early July. When he crossed the threshold, he said you could have cut the odour with a knife. It flowed down the stairs and into all the rooms, even the parlour, which, like many similar rooms of the time, contained stuffed birds in glass cases, antimacassars and china dogs on the mantlepiece, which was adorned with the customary chenille swags and finished with a bobble fringe. The parlour was only ever used at Christmas and important family gatherings, but the smell had even seeped into this sanctuary and invaded its privacy.

My father told how he walked purposefully upstairs to Uncle Henry's room, and into an atmosphere which made breathing difficult. He never spoke a word—merely pulled off the bedding and tipped the occupant on to the floor, stripped the struggling, swearing old man naked, and commanded Cousin Rene to bring the tin bath and hot water. Amid shrieks and flying fists the two of them subdued Uncle Henry, scrubbed him from top to toe, dried him, and dressed him in a clean nightshirt. Cousin Rene changed the stinking bed for clean linen, swapping the mattress for the one in the spare room, and

3

they shovelled the victim back into bed. My father levelled his bright blue eyes at the old man and commanded, in his best military manner, 'Don't you ever do that again, do you hear? You will change and wash, and if you are going to stay there till you die, you do it in a clean manner. Understand?'

Apparently the old man did understand. There was no more trouble, although he never again left his room despite the fact that he was hale and hearty. His excuse was that the Bible said man was only expected to live 'three score years and ten', and he had reached that age and expected the Lord to take him like He said He would; and anyway, he was waiting to meet up with his Amy, to ask her where she had hidden the money she had saved out of the housekeeping.

After that Cousin Rene ran the little farm singlehanded with only occasional help, getting older, thinner and more careworn as she cooked for, fed and waited on the wicked old man and coped with everything else. People did that for their parents in those days and no questions asked. The old man ate and drank in his accustomed manner, getting fatter and fatter, and eventually succumbed to a sudden heart attack.

I remember the old farm vividly, because to me as a small girl, it was absolute heaven. To reach it one had to cross several fields, as there was no road—not even a track. We always had a small car of some sort, and bounced or squelched across the permanent pasture, according to what the weather had done to it, to reach the house. The farmhouse was red-brick, the top half tile-hung, with a thatched roof, worn and inhabited by various families of birds. Some parts had slipped, and hung down crazily over the tiny leaded windows that had the appearance of small, crafty eyes peering suspiciously at the outside world.

The front door, painted green, was blistered and peeled where the hot summer sun had struck. Visiting children (myself included) loved to pop the blisters, leaving bare circles that the rain soaked through, so that inside there was a thin film of white mould. This door was only used for funerals and the like. The back door was on the north side and protected from the winds by a rickety corrugated iron porch, over which climbed a Montana clematis. This flower lent great beauty to the scene when fully out in early summer. Cousin Rene told how she had bought it as a cutting from the local flower show years before.

The house stood in the middle of the farmyard, which was enclosed by a ring fence made of post and rail, much of which had rotted away. Parts of it were broken as the result of recalcitrant cows or bolting horses. There was a big, dim cowshed with a loft over, where the sweet-scented meadow hay was stored, and an opening reached by a solid wooden ladder. It was exciting to climb up and throw down the hay to the beasts beneath. Next door was the stable with four stalls, and a continuation of the loft with another trap door. This was one of my favourite haunts, for I was always besotted with horses, and the two farm workhorses were the gentlest of beasts. I used to sit on their mangers and feed them titbits, which they took gently, with their big rubbery lips brushing my face and hair, as they crunched an apple or carrot, breathing their sweet breath over me—it was sheer bliss.

The stable was also the favourite haunt of the farmyard hens which scuttled and scuffed around from dawn to dusk, and made their nests under, and sometimes in, the mangers. One of the most exciting things was to be given a little chip basket, and sent to collect as many eggs as I could find. The nests were not only to be found in the stable, however, but in the rickyard, under the hedges, and in any dark secret place into which a hen could creep hoping to secure herself a nice clutch and then go broody and sit in peace.

Later she would appear all proud and scruffy trailing a brood of tiny fluffy chicks across the yard. The little chicks were unafraid, but I soon learned to keep out of the old hens' way, as they would have no hesitation in rushing at you and giving you a fierce peck to protect their young.

The pond, covered in green weed, was home to a few ducks and many moorhens. A lovely blue kingfisher appeared occasionally, probably from the nearby brook that meandered through the fields. I used to feed the ducks, and clad in my rubber boots, slither and slide to pick up their eggs, which they unfeelingly deposited in the muddiest places on the banks. The brook was clear and sparkling, and full of sticklebacks which hung in cloud-like packs close to the bank, and sometimes were swept downstream by a sudden rush of water. A visit to Cousin Rene always meant that the little white fishing net on its bamboo pole had to be packed. She always had a jam jar, with a string handle attached to its neck, ready for me, as well as a bag of delicious home-made buns to sustain the fisherman. I spent long and happy hours trawling for the tiny fish, returning triumphant, hungry and incredibly muddy, with my catch.

The stackyard was a lovely place. Here stood the trim hayricks and straw stacks, each roughly thatched against the weather, and all invaded by a multitude of rats and mice. Oh, the fun of a day's ratting with old Spot the terrier, whose keen eye and flashing teeth put paid to many an unwary rodent.

Perhaps the most mysterious place, and one of the most thrilling, was the granary: up four steps and push open the creaking door. With only one window, covered in cobwebs hanging with feed dust, the inside was dark and warm and deadly exciting. It was perched up on staddle stones, those mushroom-like creations which have been bought at inflated prices in recent years by Yuppies to decorate their dreadful 'patios'.

Although this barn was raised off the ground to stop vermin getting in, they always found a way, and as the door opened the sound of skittering feet, as the pests bolted for the escape routes, made a delicious shiver run down my spine. Perhaps a feel for milling came with the genes from my paternal line, for I loved the smells of the granary: bran and oats, maize and wheat, and all the feeds now long abandoned, sharps and middlings, barley meal and flake maize, chick feed, linseed, molasses—a wonderful smell of plenty. There was a pop hole in the door to let the farm cats in to sort the rodents out. It was also an entry for the hens, who could be seen sedately negotiating the steps and stooping through the hole to steal a nest on a pile of West of England sacks, or in an old bucket, and at the conclusion of a successful visit, bursting out of the hole with a succession of raucous squawks of triumph, flying in a wide arc from the top of the steps far into the yard, and then, with a ruffle of feathers, running off to join the rest of the flock, proclaiming the glad news of another egg to all who cared to listen. There were pigs in sties, a small flock of sheep, and some twelve cows, milked, of course, by hand. When I was around seven it was Cousin Rene who showed me the correct method of abstracting milk from the reluctant bovines, a skill I appreciated in later years.

How Cousin Rene got through all the work she did is a mystery. At the time I was too young to appreciate her efforts. In spite of accomplishing all the milking, feeding of stock, carting of hay, mucking out and the like, there were always home-cured and cooked hams, home-made cakes, pies and bread, jams and pickles lovingly made by her busy hands. In the little brick dairy I loved to help turn the handle of the separator, and watch the cream come out of one spout, and the skimmed milk out of the other. 'How does the cream know which spout to come out of, Cousin Rene?' I asked, and she would smile and wrinkle her tired eyes and say, 'Ah, that's a secret magic.'

The butter churn also worked a secret magic. Why, I wondered, did the butter come quickly on some days, and not on others? 'It's the climate,' explained Cousin Rene. I was not sure what climate was, and thought it might be some elf or other outsider who had climbed into the churn as they did in my fairy stories. The cream on our newly-baked bread at teatime was spread half an inch deep over the strawberry jam, and the ham, cut thick and with a good bit of fat, was part of old Jolly, the pig, that I had fed with swill and barley meal on my last visit. It did not worry me, as being a country child, I was brought up on the premise that if you serve animals well, they will serve you well, and that included providing a good meal.

Some of the eggs I had collected would be boiled, and served with the ham, and hot, dark tea came in Cousin Rene's best porcelain china that had been a wedding gift to her mother. It was always brought out for the benefit of my mother who liked nice things. Uncle Henry did not hold with such things as fine china, and took his beverages in an enormous willow pattern cup, pouring the tea into the saucer, and swilling it down with loud sucking noises. This caused my mother to look askance and his daughter to exclaim: 'Really father, must you do that?' A remonstrance to which the old man paid not the slightest bit of attention.

I once went up to see Uncle Henry after he had taken to his bed, and asked him why he did not get up and come out in the sun and give me a ride on old Rosie's broad back, like he used to. He squinted at me with my father's blue eyes, and replied shortly that the 'time had come to put away earthly joys.' I did not understand what he meant, but my father said crisply that Uncle Henry spent far too much time reading the Bible.

Our visits to the farm ceased when we moved to live in East Anglia, and I never saw Cousin Rene again. I often wonder how long she battled on for survival. But most of all I would dearly love to know if, when Uncle Henry finally went to the other world, he met his Amy, and whether she let on where she had hidden the housekeeping money. If she did—what did he do about it?

CHAPTER TWO

There was a time when my grandfather, that is my mother's father, kept a large number of snakes in a greenhouse, but my grandmother put a stop to that after the odd-jobman put one in the cook's bed, and sent the poor woman shrieking into the night. Good cooks were hard to come by at that time. Gramps then acquired two anteaters, and all went well until one, no doubt keen to get at the ants he was serving them for dinner, clawed his arm badly. While he was in hospital enjoying the rough and ready surgery of Victorian times, the offending animals were sent away. After that he contented himself with the humble horse: carriage and hunting varieties. He roared about all over the Glamorganshire countryside on a 17 hands high creature, either jumping unjumpable fences, or falling off into the dirtiest ditches. Dogs were his constant companions, from the giant English Mastiff and Great Danes, which he exhibited at shows in Wales in the 1880s with some success, to the Curly Coated retrievers which accompanied him shooting. I gathered he was not over-struck on my grandmother's pug dog.

All the family were crazy about fancy fowls, and numerous aunts and uncles exhibited these all over the country. Great Aunt Rose, it was said, shampooed her hens in a silver bowl placed on the Chinese carpet before the drawingroom fire by the butler—they did things in style in Victorian days. My grandfather, however, kept his poultry in a much more businesslike way undertaking his preparation for shows in one of the outbuildings. On reflection, this was probably on orders from my grandmother, who had perforce to keep a close eye on the more hair-brained schemes her spouse entertained.

My first recollections of my mother's parents are in the mid '20s when they had moved to Foxhill, a house in a country district of Berkshire. In those days it was all girt about with lovely heather-clad commons, and deep woods with little pools full of tadpoles in spring. The whole countryside was garlanded with flowers. The house, which always seemed large to a small child, was in fact of moderate size. The garden, of something approaching an acre, had mysterious shrubberies, and old stables with a huge high loft. There was also a deserted tack room that still had wooden pegs for harness and collars on the walls, and various other dusty and exciting places.

My grandfather's enthusiasm for fancy poultry and rabbits was at its height at this time. The property boasted a small meadow, and neat poultry houses with runs, hopefully fox-proof, dotting the perimeter. In the centre the rabbits, or some of them, lived in cages based on the fashionable 'Morant' system. These were long hutches with a wooden-floored sleeping compartment, and a wire-floored run. The hutches had two handles at either end and could be easily moved twice daily on to fresh grazing. In late April all the rabbits were moved back into the loft, where some 30 to 40 does and selected bucks of the Blue Beveran variety lived in great luxury. The meadow was chain-harrowed and shut up for the grass to grow. In late June we made hay, and this, stacked in a neat rick by the hedge, kept the rabbits supplied through the winter.

My grandfather was one of the best of the species: he always had time for his grandchildren, my older stepsister, myself and my two cousins, whom he loved dearly, and instructed us in the ways of the countryside and animal husbandry with patience and diligence. On attaining the age of seven years we were taught to handle a gun and to shoot with the long-barrelled ·410. All four of us became very good shots. I possibly spent more time than the others with my grandfather: my stepsister was grown-up and pursuing her theatrical career, and my two male cousins were at public school. I was lucky that, whenever my father and mother had a financial crisis, which was pretty often, Daddy went back to Bristol, and Mother and I went to Foxhill. At times, when one or both of the grandparents were ill enough to need a supportive offspring, it was my mother, and not her brother or sister, who was sent for. She was the most practical and the best nurse, and also, with her kind heart, the most likely to drop everything and respond to a summons, and we would reside there until the invalid recovered.

After my father was killed in an accident when I was 11, we spent considerably more time at Foxhill, and once lived there for nearly a year; so I had ample time to absorb all the interesting things Gramps was willing to teach me. I learned how to prepare and box up the poultry and rabbits for transport to the shows, and how to label boxes securely, not forgetting to put Gramps' address on the reverse side of the label, so that it could be turned over and re-affixed to the box for the return journey. Every week the local carrier called with his horse and covered-wagon-type vehicle (this was not replaced by a motorised van until the end of the '20s) to take the exhibits to the station at Reading for dispatch all over the country. We waited with excitement as they were conveyed back by the carrier, and carefully decanted at the back gate. There was the thrill of unboxing, and looking in the slot inside the lid to find how many prize cards, and of what denomination, the creature had collected at the show.

This early training in exhibiting infected me with a 'showing bug' from which I have suffered all my life. I have exhibited everything from dogs and ponies to rabbits, goats, flowers, produce and even, once, my young daughter, who won a glass sugar bowl for her healthy looks, but failed to get placed in the class as the doctor said she was too fat!

Gramps had an intense love of fires and explosions, and no doubt it was my early exposure to these elements that caused my devotion to them to this day. When the old man knew that my mother and myself were coming to stay, he saved all the burnable matter in a big heap, getting John, the garden boy, to cover it with sacks to keep it dry until we arrived. On the second day of each visit, with the assistance of John, he made a huge bonfire, and instructed me in the correct method of making pyres that would catch easily. I was allowed to light them with a long paper spill ignited by my grandfather, from one of a box of Swan Vestas matches kept for such a purpose, as well as for lighting his sweet-smelling pipe. Once the sticks caught fire the flames roared upward in a most satisfactory manner. We kept piling on the branches and rubbish until the heap was reduced to a smoking rubble, and then happily trotted indoors for tea.

The greatest thrill, until the local authorities and my grandmother (both spoilsports, we considered) put a stop to it, was the blowing up of unwanted tree stumps. Mature pine trees on the common were always blowing down in gales, leaving their great, earth-encrusted roots sticking up in the air. The authorities sold the trunks, which were sawn through and carted away by the contractors, while lesser men bought and carried off the branches. This left the roots, full of good firewood, and my grandfather bought these for a song. In order to break them up quickly, so that John could barrow the pieces back to the house, my grandfather had the ingenious idea of blowing the roots apart. He had accomplished this successfully on one stump and one autumn when we went to stay, it was to learn that he had saved the second explosion for my visit.

Was it easier to get dynamite in the 1920s I wonder? Anyway, Gramps had a box of sticks which he kept in the safe in his study, and one morning we set off to the common up the road with dynamite, caps and fuse, together with John, the wheelbarrow and a large handsaw for the awkward bits. Gramps was a whizz at setting a charge and allowed me to light the fuse, and then we all ran for cover behind a gorse bush some distance away. **Bang**! the whole thing blew up with a marvellous noise, showering lumps of root and earth over a wide distance, some of it falling on us. It was a most satisfactory morning, and John was kept trotting back and forth with barrow loads of wood for two days.

After two more such satisfactory explosions, a local do-gooder complained and said we were a danger and a nuisance, and some authority told Gramps he had to stop blowing up things on common land. However, he was not that easily put off a ploy which he considered a good, as well as amusing, exercise; so he commissioned a local farmer with two horses to put chains on the next stump and haul it back to the house. This was done, and there the enormous and unsightly thing sat, on the site of the bonfire, much to my grandmother's chagrin.

I was not there when the first stump not 'in situ' was exploded, but apparently all went well, and in spite of rattling the windows a bit, no damage was done. I was, however, back for the next and last explosion. This was a pretty big root, and it had taken all the strength of the two horses to get it off the common and down the road, and then through the farm gate on to the accustomed spot for disintegration. My grandfather decided that as the stump was so large he had better put in two charges, one each side, and this he did. I lighted one fuse and he lighted the other and the usual scuttle for cover took place. It was a magnificent explosion, the noise was deafening, a multitude of lumps of wood sailed through the air; unfortunately, one sailed right through the window of the bedroom in which my mother and I slept and buried itself in the ceiling. There was also the little matter of the tiles off the stable roof and the broken kitchen window, to say nothing of the filthy appearance of the chief participants. Grandmother put her dainty foot down as firmly as only she could: it was, sadly, the end of a great adventure.

I think my grandfather would have made an excellent poacher; indeed he practised the art in a small way and it gave him a good chuckle. He was adept at setting all kinds of traps and snares, from the humble wooden mousetrap, the wire snare, and the sparrow cage, to the gin trap, then legal but now banned. Rodents of all sorts abounded and wreaked havoc on his large and flourishing vegetable and fruit garden and in chicken pen and rabbit hutch. Every night the mousetraps were set at intervals under the eight foot laurel hedge that divided the vegetable garden from the lane, gins were set in runways to catch rats, and along the meadow hedge a few wire snares for the superabundance of rabbits. I learned how to set the snares and traps successfully without getting my fingers caught, although I was never allowed, until in my teens, to set the gins which were lethal and could break an unwary finger. Each morning we were out early to spring the empty traps. This was to stop the robins and other songbirds getting caught, and to take a tally of the rats, mice and rabbits that had walked unwarily during the hours of darkness.

Any wild rabbits snared had to be paunched, another job I learned to do, slitting the belly from breastbone down, cleaning out the entrails and depositing them in the manure pit. The rabbits were then hung in the cool cellar for a few days before making a delicious rabbit pie or stew. Every Saturday night the traps were left unset: Gramps did not hold with hunting, shooting, fishing or even trapping on the Sabbath, although after supper each Sunday night we reset the traps. Possibly, the old man imagined that nothing was going to get itself caught until after midnight!

Some of our snares, I regret to say, got set in the farmer's field behind the garden, but he never said anything, and several pheasants that fed there appeared on our dinner table.

Foxhill was an apt name for the house as it was on a hill and the foxes were an absolute plague. If you got up at first light (fox light it was called in some country places) and looked out of the bedroom window overlooking the farmer's field, you could watch the foxes trotting back to the woodlands behind it, keeping in close to the dividing hedge, some even with a hen in their jaws. Gramps was always losing poultry to the foxes in spite of all precautions, and several times the rabbit hutches were torn apart and the inmates taken. Rats would get into hutches and kill baby rabbits, steal the eggs from the nests, attack the young chicks, and even kill a hen if she defended her nest. When a rat ran through the hen run in daytime there would be a frightful commotion as the hens all banded together to chase it, and if they cornered it, would attack it fiercely. The same thing often happened to unwary mice.

Gramps was a keen gardener, and his rows of vegetables, each in its prescribed season, plantations of currant bushes, raspberry and loganberry canes, cherry trees and the huge strawberry patch, together with the apple and greengage trees and an enormous profusion of rhubarb, supplied the house all year round. Much was bottled or turned into preserves and pickles.

Surplus produce was sold at Reading market on Saturday, and Friday was busy and fun as we spent from early morning until dusk, picking, sorting and packing any soft fruit or vegetables in season—red, black and white currants, herbs, tomatoes and apples. Any visitors were marched out to do their stint at harvesting. Vegetables were weighed, and bunched or packed in punnets or chip baskets, and eggs put into dozens in tissue-paper-lined boxes. Most of the apples, except in a year of super abundance were stored on racks in one of the old barns. Early on Saturday morning the carrier called and collected all the goods and took them to market, and Gramps, wearing his best russet-coloured Harris tweed knickerbocker suit, with cap to match and shining brown shoes, caught the bus to town and attended the auction. When he returned for the ritual drawing room tea at four o'clock, we could judge the success, or otherwise, of our efforts by his face: a satisfied smirk when prices were good, or a down-turned lip when the sale had been poor. All the monies thus received went into his fund for buying seed, or animal food, and I learned how to balance a budget and come out on the right side.

Although at Foxhill there was no farm stock as such to interest me, my wandering around the village and its outlying farms provided me with food for thought. In an old red-brick thatched cottage behind the belt of pines that separated it from the little mission church and the road to Reading, lived a very strange old lady. Her name was Miss Vyner and she kept all manner of animals including a large number of goats which she tethered about the village. There were various tales about her: one was that she was the daughter of an aristocratic house. Whether this was true I have no idea, but she was an educated woman with a low and well-modulated voice and impeccable manners.

I struck up a friendship with this odd character, who was delighted when I told her how Cousin Rene had taught me to milk, and she allowed me to practise on the nannies. Her method of milking was to sit on her three-legged stool, behind the goat, who would straddle her legs thus making it quite easy to milk into the little pail as goats only have two teats, one on each side. Miss Vyner said that was how they milked the sheep in Switzerland and she found it worked well with the goats. I quickly adopted this novel seat, and my milking technique improved greatly.

I found Miss Vyner very kind and not at all deserving of the nickname 'the old witch' bestowed on her by the village children, who shouted out rather rude things as they passed the gate to her garden. They could, however, be excused to some extent because she certainly looked a bit like a witch with her brown, wrinkled, whiskery-chinned face, sharp, black eyes, and straggly grey hair hanging down under an old, greasy, black trilby with the crown punched up. She was clad in a brown cardigan full of holes, a stuff blouse, and a thick tweed skirt over which a West of England sack was tied about her waist with binder twine, to serve as a protective apron. The ensemble was completed by a pair of men's hobnailed boots, and it has to be said that she smelt very strongly of billy goat.

Miss Vyner's cottage was dim and the beams were hung with herbs to dry and sides of salted pork. There were a great number of shelves housing books of all sorts, and a small desk was deep in papers covered in her spidery handwriting. Several cats lay silently on chairs or on the windowsill and a little white, black-patched terrier with cunning eyes trotted beside her; it was spoken of as a 'terror with rats.'

I was always welcomed in and fed honey cake and goat's milk; I did not much like the latter but was too polite to say so, and waited until she had gone out of the room on some errand before hastily pouring it out of the window or into a convenient flower pot.

At the age of 10 I was developing an enquiring mind. Every time I went to visit Miss Vyner there were more kids, sucking greedily from their browsing mothers. One day I summoned up enough courage to ask the 64,000 dollar question: 'Miss Vyner, how do you get so many baby goats?' She looked at me quizzically and replied in a matter of fact voice: 'Well dear, I put the nanny with billy and he gives her a couple of embraces and we get another kid.' The answer satisfied me, as I did not understand the implication, having been kept very free of all matters of a sexual nature. However, I went back full of this new information and blurted it out in a delighted manner at teatime in the drawing room. There was a horrified silence as Granny's eyes and my mother's met and

21

their brows raised. They said something urgently to each other in French, which they always used when they did not want me to understand, and turned sharply on my grandfather who was chuckling as if he thought it a great joke.

Later I was informed that Miss Vyner was talking nonsense, and that I was to forget all about it. What was more, I was forbidden ever to go near her again. 'Forbidden' meant just that—so another opening in my farming career was closed for a time.

CHAPTER THREE

It was old Jack the ploughman who got me banned from
farm visits for quite some time. I was eight and we were
living in Essex, and joy of joys, next to a farm where,
needless to say, I spent all my spare time. The farmhouse
was enormous, with a marvellous kitchen housing a great
black range, a bread oven, and several old arm chairs and a
sofa full of cats and dogs of various sizes and ages. The
farmer's wife was a fat, jolly woman whose children had
grown up; two sons worked on the farm, and she was
happy to have a spare child under her feet again. The
farmyard was extensive with huge barns and stables, and a
cowshed that held fifty at milking. There was a piggery, a
large flock of sheep, and poultry everywhere. However,
my joy was in the big farm horses; six of them, who drew
the ploughs, the waggons and harrows, and worked
patiently all hours and in all weathers. Duke and Duchess,
the pair used by Jack for much of the important work,
were my particular favourites.

Jack was a lean old man, with a creased face, wind-
scorched cheeks, and faded-grey eyes. He was never
encountered without an ancient and vile-smelling pipe in
the corner of his mouth. His garb consisted of worn and
greasy cord trousers tied under the knee with bits of

binder twine referred to as 'yorks'. These kept the bottoms up out of the mud and, when in the barn, the rats from running up inside a trouser leg. His feet were encased in large black hobnailed boots. His outfit was finished off with a collarless grey flannel shirt with a white bone stud in front. His worn old jacket with torn pockets held everything from a white-spotted red handkerchief, a tobacco pouch and matches, to twine, nails, a huge clasp knife, harness buckles, old bootlaces, any number of undefinable objects and a bag of peppermints of which he, I and the horses were inordinately fond. His old cap was greasy and worn, and he carried a khaki canvas bag over his shoulder that contained his mid-day meal: the heel of a loaf, a large lump of cheese and a bottle of cold tea. All of these he would willingly share with anyone present, carving chunks off both bread and cheese with the not-very-clean clasp knife that had probably last been used on the horses' hoofs or to paunch a rabbit caught in the field by his old lurcher Mary. She slunk round the hedges while he worked, always bringing any catch back to her master in a manner more reminiscent of a well-trained retriever. Those were some of the best meals I ever shared.

Jack had endless grown-up children and many grand-children and adopted me as an extra. When I ran down the fields after school to cadge a ride on one of the horses, usually one or more of his grandchildren came too, and we all rode back, sometimes three to a horse, singing 'Uncle Tom Cobley' at the top of our voices.

In the summer holidays I escaped from home and sped

into the farmyard as soon as I could, with my mother's warning of, 'Don't be a nuisance. Don't get into mischief. Mind you don't tear your dress again,' and 'Be home in time for lunch/tea' ringing in my ears.

Jack would have gone down to the fields at daybreak with Duke and Duchess. In the early spring he was busy about the ploughing on the bare brown fields. He was a wonderful countryman, and would be eager to tell any child or assembled children, who followed him like the Pied Piper's band, about the plovers who laid their eggs on the bare earth, and how he had often stopped the horses and moved the nest to another furrow, so as not to destroy the eggs. He also told tales of the Hunt which crossed the land. 'They don't catch many of they foxes,' he would chuckle, 'but they'se a mort useful for movin' 'em about. Foxes 'll pack if they can, and then look out they as 'as poultry.'

In winter the thrilling sounds of the horn and the cry of the hounds were to be heard across the fields, and one Saturday when I and several of Jack's grandchildren were up watching him harrowing, the hunt came past, hounds in full cry and horses mud stained and sweating, at the gallop. The exciting scent of hot horse and the speed of their passing raised a cheer from the group of children, and later, when Charlie Fox stole out of a copse nearby Jack pulled the horses up and we had the thrill of seeing him raise his cap and give a spirited view-holla in his cracked old voice.

Hunting finished before the breeding season started, and by then the seeding was done, and the fields shut up

25

for hay. Haymaking and harvesting meant that you rode squealing for joy on top of the loads as they went back to the farm, rattled back to the field in the empty waggon, teeth chattering with the friction of iron-shod wheels on hard-baked ruts, and at the end of the day, rode back in triumph on the sweaty back of old Duchess.

My mother, who was very proper, had not banked on the only child of her second marriage turning out to be a tomboy, and did not really approve of my goings-on. Daddy was absent quite a lot of the time, 'travelling' they said; I found out that meant trying to sell things to people who probably did not want them, but I am sure he succeeded quite well, for I overheard one of his friends say to Mother, 'Harry could sell ice to the Eskimos.' At the time I wondered whether he was indeed up there in the snow and cold doing just that; but when he came home he was not wearing a fur hood and did not have frostbite like the hero in the adventure story I read, who almost gave his all to save someone's child. Mother vainly tried to keep me in but the call of the farm was too strong, and although I promised not to be away long, I always broke the promise as I did not have a watch so had a good excuse for my tardiness.

Egg collecting was again a job for me. As there were more hens than on Uncle Henry's farm there were more eggs, and these were found in barns and sheds all over the farm. I used to collect them in a bucket, and when I had brought in three or four half-bucketfuls, which was all I could carry, I was given a big glass of home-made lemonade and a wedge of rich currant cake as a reward, making me less hungry for the meal mother had prepared and causing another scene.

There was a fairly large staff on the farm, from the dairymaid to the shepherd; who like all of his kind, was a taciturn man, but when he smiled his face lit up like the dawn. They spoiled all the children that swarmed about, and we took turns to ride old Cherry, one of the short-horn cows, in for milking, although her bony back was not nearly as comfortable as Duchess's. Once I was hoisted up on old Nellie, the large white sow, who was a peaceful soul unless she had a litter of piglets, when she was a holy terror and once bit the pigman's leg right through his boot. Pigs are not good rides as they are so prickly and once was enough!

Jack's domain was the harness room, where all the tack was kept and cleaned and the brasses polished until they shone like the sun. If the horses had to take a waggon to market they had their manes and tails braided and decorated with straw and coloured ribbons. It was Jack who taught me how to plait a mane, and I would be perched up on the back of old Duchess, working away with my nimble fingers until they were quite sore. When we had done, Jack would light the old primus stove with much hissing and spluttering of the jet, and boil water in a blackened kettle, making strong tea in an old brown teapot, pouring it out into two chipped enamel mugs—it was delicious.

However, it was Jack and Duchess who brought my farming career to a full stop for a time and it happened like this: Daddy was due home for tea and I had promised faithfully to be in by three o'clock, so that I could be cleaned up. But at that hour I was still up the fields with Jack and the horses, and it was not until 4:30 that our procession entered the farmyard. The two horses, with me perched up on Duchess, made straight for the water trough as they always did on getting back. I leaned over Duchess's neck when Jack undid the belly band and pulled off the cart saddle and breeching, and watched while he did the same for Duke. The horses still had on their heavy collars with the big metal hames and their blinkered bridles, the bits hanging down on one side having been unbuckled so they could drink comfortably. What caused the ruckus is unclear, but suddenly Duke flung up his head, his collar slapped back on his neck and a point of the hames hit Duchess a crack on her cheek. She leapt to one side, wheeled round and made off at a flat gallop for the dark, looming doorway of the stable. At that inopportune moment my father strode into the yard.

I can still remember the speed with which that dark cavern advanced towards me, and more by instinct for self-preservation than any knowledge of how to deal with such a situation I clasped the old mare's neck tightly with my arms—horse and rider arrived unharmed and with an abrupt stop in the right stall. Oh dear the fuss! My father lost his considerable temper, the farmer's wife flew out of the door at the sound of the raised voice, the farmer himself came running from a barn, dogs barked, and hens, ducks and geese scattered as farmhands ran to gather round the combatants. I, still seated on my old friend and excited about the whole adventure, turned round so that I was back-to-front on the mare's ample rump, and listened to the uproar, wondering just what punishment I was going to receive. It was the worst of all: we would move house, I could not be trusted to stay away from the farm (too right—I could not!) so we would leave the vicinity at once. My parents were fed up with my predilection for spending all my days getting muddy and tearing my dresses, and coming home smelling of animals and so on and so on. I was not even allowed to say goodbye.

The cottage we were living in was only rented. It was given up, and, horror of horrors, the next home was a house in Stowmarket—a town of all things. Mother told me that the poet Milton had once lived in the house, composing *Paradise Lost* while seated under the old mulberry tree: that I was to have a governess and lessons with the vicar's daughter Monica, who wore a brace on her teeth; and that I could have the two rabbits my grandfather would send me, as well as a tortoise and a black cat (and there were mother's Yorkshire Terriers) but definitely—*no farms*! It was poor exchange for old Jack and Duchess.

CHAPTER FOUR

It was the Locking family who made me realise how sensitive people can be and how easily they can take umbrage. Up to then I had thought all people were marvellous, and at 15 I remember throwing wide my arms and exclaiming joyfully: 'The whole world is my friend!' The Lockings opened my eyes to how wrong I was.

My father had departed this life some four years previously, and mother and I were existing in a small cottage in Sussex, desperately hard up but keeping up appearances. My mother, who had been born into a well-to-do Victorian family, never forgot her upbringing, although adult life had not treated her very generously. One disastrous marriage when she was 21 and a hastily contracted second one to my father in 1918, when her kind heart fell for the wounded officer back from the trenches, had resulted in many buffets along life's way. Money or lack of it was always a problem, but I in the euphoric state of being young, fit and ready for anything, was blissfully ignorant of the cruelties of life, as girls of my age and upbringing mostly were in the early 1930s.

We had not long moved to the cottage when I went in search of hens to buy. I had always been allowed to keep hens and rabbits, as well as numerous cats and dogs, wherever we were living, and we moved frequently. I longed for a horse, but that was out of the question. The village postmistress advised me to see Mr Locking who lived in the council houses at the bottom of our lane, as he did casual work for many of the local farmers and would be sure to know where there were hens for sale. I called at the Locking house one evening, knocking loudly on the door, and greeted the child who opened it with a bright smile. It was a boy of about 10 in short tweed trousers, much patched, cut knees and a runny nose. He agreed to 'fetch me dad.' 'Me Dad' was tall and muscular with a depressingly low hairline and heavy brows which gave him a Neanderthal appearance. He was not a talkative man, and when I asked if he knew of any hens for sale, he grunted: 'Farmer Thompson, up the lane,' jerking his thumb in the relevant direction—and promptly slammed the door in my face.

Hooper's Farm, where Farmer Thompson lived, was a picturesque Sussex farmhouse, all warm red-brick and with a brightly coloured flower garden kept in great order, I found out later, by his old mother who also lived there. I bought six hens at four shillings each, which cleaned out my money box, and conned Mr Thompson into giving me a bag of corn for free. I asked about the farm, and if I could sometimes come and help, preferably with the horses, and he said I could come up if I liked as long as I 'did not get in the way.' I was rather annoyed about this as it sounded as if he was treating me like a child. The hens took up residence in the old shed in the garden, and prospered on the free corn and scraps, and in a few weeks, when they had recovered from the change in their lives, started laying large brown eggs.

I got a job with a very rich woman who bred and exhibited Siamese cats; my tasks included changing and washing cat blankets, preparing their meals and emptying their litter trays. The ten shillings a week I earned for five and a half days' labour helped with housekeeping and hen food. After only a week my employer offered to give me a three year old 'queen', as the female cat is called. I was delighted, especially when she said I could have a free stud service to one of her champions when the cat (I called her Pinklepurr) was calling. No sooner was Pinklepurr installed in the cottage than she immediately started calling. Those who are familiar with the loud voices of the breed will have some idea of the noise she made. In spite of tight security, she escaped and later produced a litter of black kittens! My employer was not pleased and insisted the kittens be got rid of, and that as soon as Pinklepurr was calling again I was to take her immediately to the cattery for service. I had imagined the cat was mine, but I was wrong.

My employer's bidding was done. As soon as Pinklepurr called again I took her back to the cattery. She was mated to the champion cat and in due course produced one tom kitten. When it was six weeks old my employer arrived at my home in her chauffeur-driven Daimler and said she had come to collect the kitten. 'But it's mine,' I protested. 'Of course not, you stupid girl,' she snorted. 'I did not charge you a stud fee, you owe me a kitten, it's just a pity there is only one.' 'Well, if that is how you feel,'

I retorted, 'you had better take Pinklepurr back as well.' And she did. Consolation prize—the kitten which I had bred grew up to become a champion.

A well-known Sunday newspaper sent a photographer to take pictures of the cats as Siamese were then rare. My employer posed, as prettily as a middle-aged, dumpy redhead can, with the champions, but they used instead a picture of me with an armful of kittens. My employer was so mad she sacked me. This was annoying as it was not even a very good picture!

To celebrate my freedom I bought a setting of eggs, put them under one of the hens who had gone broody and she hatched me twelve chicks, nine of which turned out to be cocks.

The summer was long and hot, and I spent quite a bit of it up at Hooper's Farm supposedly helping with the haymaking, but really only useful to take trace horses back and forth to the fields—just the job as I could ride them. Mr Locking was employed for the summer but he seldom spoke much and certainly not to me.

In the autumn my Mother was asked if she would produce a pantomime for the Women's Institute: word had got round that she had theatrical connections—well she had, briefly, to be sure: a walk-on at Drury Lane in 'The Whip', and as an exhibition tango dancer with a partner at one of the big London hotels during the war. Most of the stardust was thrown around by my stepsister, 19 years my senior, who had been in repertory since she was 15 and came home with hilarious stories of life in digs and the provincial theatres of the time.

Mother had many talents and one of them proved to be as a producer of pantomimes. As she was also an artist of some merit, she designed and painted the canvas backdrops for the stage in the village hall with the help of a few locals. A chorus was a necessity for such an enterprise— mother held auditions. Among the hopefuls were the whole family of Lockings: six girls and two boys. A lady who had lived all her life in the village advised my mother to take on the girls as Mrs L. was an accomplished needlewoman and would help with the costumes, but not to have the boys at any price as they were a menace to the village and would be sure to upset everything. 'Say you have no parts for boys,' she said looking wise, and closing one eye. The result was six smirking Locking girls and six other assorted maidens. The two Locking boys hung around outside the village hall during rehearsals, catcalling the girls, and once dropped a stink bomb behind the WI President when she came to see how things were progressing.

I too, had my moment of being starstruck and ended up doubling the parts of the Knave of Hearts and the Fairy Queen, the latter appearing only briefly in Scene One for which I was duly thankful: it was not my joy to be wreathed in white net with a star on my head, I was far more at home in the Knave's doublet and hose. The rehearsals proceeded apace, and things were coming to a splendid climax with the actual show only 10 days away, when I found out how tetchy people can be and quite innocently threw a spanner in the carefully oiled works. It was after rehearsal one night and as we all streamed out, the Locking girls in a pack passed me accompanied by their grim-faced mother. 'Goodnight Lockings,' I called out gaily as I made for the cottage.

Next day my mother received a curt note written on a dirty piece of paper torn from an exercise book: 'Dear Madam, Me and my girls wont be taking no more part in your pantermine. S. Locking.' Mother was devastated. 'Whyever should they want to leave?' she exclaimed. 'What can I do? I can't train six new girls in less than two weeks!' That evening she sallied forth to see the Locking family. Mr Locking opened the door. 'Can I come in?' my mother asked. 'No you can't,' he retorted, 'we don't want no more to do with your family treatin' my wife like that.' 'Like what?' My mother was bewildered. 'Your snooty daughter,' he answered angrily, 'calling my missus "Locking" and no missus before 'er name, who do she think we is, 'er servants?' My mother came home and taxed me with the crime. I had to admit that I had called out, but I meant it for all the family, no disrespect. Mother went back again and explained. No explanation or apology would be accepted; they had been slighted, or thought they had, and that was that. I then knew for sure that the whole world was not my friend, and that perhaps I had better be a bit more careful what I said in future and to whom I said it. If only I had remembered and heeded this early warning I might not have got in some of the spots in which I have since found myself.

Mother, the most resourceful person I have ever known, dragooned six wretched women, including plump Cissy from behind the post office counter and the young butcher's wife, to join the chorus, gave them a crash course of lessons in singing and dancing, and adjusted the already Locking-made costumes to fit some of the more ample figures. The pantomime was a rip-roaring success, and we were requested to take it to several outlying villages.

The nine cockerels that I had hatched grew into fine plump birds, but although we needed them to eke out our menu, mother would not think of dining off anything she had known personally during its growing period. However, in the village lived a wonderful old character who reared and sold table poultry to a number of houses in the neighbourhood. I had a bright idea. 'I'll take one of the birds down to Mrs Curtis,' I told my mother, 'and swap it for one of hers, you'll eat that won't you?' Mother agreed that would be fine as she would not have had even a nodding acquaintance with one of Mrs Curtis's cockerels. So off I went with one of my birds under my arm, and explained the dilemma to the old lady—and my solution. She folded her hands across her ample bosom encased in a flowery pinafore and laughed till the tears ran down her fat pink cheeks. ''Tis the best joke I heard this week!' she chuckled. We dispatched my cockerel and I feathered and cleaned him. She dressed him in her own way, finishing him off with a bunch of herbs tucked under each wing, and was still chuckling when, after a cup of tea and slice of home-made sponge cake, I went off home. Mother was delighted. 'Mrs Curtis does rear lovely birds,' she said putting on her glasses to examine next day's dinner, and she enjoyed it as much as I did. The other eight birds were treated the same way, and mother never ever knew she was eating and enjoying home-reared stock!

Between our cottage and the road to town was our sloping flower garden bordered by a stream in which the occasional trout lingered. My stepsister went fishing with a bent pin and a piece of string when she stayed with us, and once caught a small fish which we divided for supper. Across from the stream was the back of the red-brick chapel where a religious sect worshipped each Sunday, the sound of their melodious singing wafting over our garden. Attached to the chapel were their living quarters, and then the village shop which they ran with great neatness and precision. They were a secret people in their warm brown habits, always kindly and softly spoken and nothing was ever any trouble. They baked their own bread, it was the best in the world, large fluffy loaves that melted in the mouth. As we were usually hard up, bread was our staple diet with our eggs and vegetables and meat bought with produce I sold, but mostly the bread was eaten with plum jam mother had made from the fruit in our garden. We, well I, must have consumed dozens of those delicious loaves during our sojourn in the village.

My dream of being a farmer was always present, and I spent my evenings working out a wonderful scheme with maps, charts and graphs, of the chain of farms I would one day own. They would be based all over England producing pork in Wiltshire, cream in Devon, eggs in Bucks, vegetables in East Anglia, beef in Hereford and so on. I would have a fleet of lorries labelled Sunset Farms Ltd taking my produce to outlets all over the country.

Looking back I think I was ahead of my time!

My visits to Hooper's farm continued, and I earned a few shillings doing various rather mean jobs like mucking out or sweeping the sheds clear of cobwebs ready for whitewashing. My smallholding efforts were confined to a few rabbits, the garden and the hens. In the spring of my sixteenth year mother bought me a pen of 12 purebred white Wyandotte pullets. Farmer Thompson allowed me to use a good-sized house and run in the paddock oppo-site, and I spent hours just standing and admiring my flock. When they were just over six months old they began to lay, small eggs at first, gradually increasing in size to large creamy beauties, the surplus of which I was able to sell. They were just in full lay when disaster struck. I went early one morning to let them out and feed them, but when I opened the henhouse door a scene of terrible carnage met my eyes. In the night a fox had ripped a board off the house and got in, and as is the habit of his kind had killed every hen and taken just one for his supper. I spread the poor mutilated bodies on the grass and wept bitter tears over them. I knew how difficult it had been for mother to afford them in the first place, how she had denied herself things in order to buy them for me, and how I had treasured them.

The Hunt was telephoned and they sent the gentleman who attended to the 'poultry fund'. He examined the birds, sympathising greatly with the bereaved, agreed it was the work of a fox, and paid me six shillings a carcass compensation. That was usual in those days when so much of the poultry lived out and was vulnerable: the local hunts were supposed to control the fox population and if they did not, they paid compensation to any who lost poultry through the depredations of foxes. In this day and age when most hens live in battery cages and table poultry languishes in darkened broiler houses, there is no need for a poultry fund any more. The loss of my poor hens depressed both my mother and me and soon after that we left the village.

CHAPTER FIVE

My mother and I continued to move between Foxhill and various rented homes throughout the 1930s. Money was scarce, at times non-existent, and how my mother managed to feed us and keep up appearances is still a mystery. Our lack of financial support meant that we had to use our ingenuity to survive, and in those days there was ample opportunity for this, as England was not strangled by all the petty rules and regulations which abound in our present 'Nanny' state, which would rather pay people to be idle than encourage them to use their native energy and wit.

My mother was a most practical and talented woman, full of ideas and determination. Unfortunately, she had no head for handling money so that when a little did come along it soon trickled away again. In 1937 we rented a bungalow in a village in Hampshire. This was on the main road to Winchester and my mother soon saw the possibility of selling refreshment to the passing motorist. One front room was quickly converted into an attractive tearoom, chairs and tables of varying sizes and condition being purchased for a few coppers at a local auction room and painted white, and some placed on the front lawn. My mother designed a pretty sign and we were in business. Her cakes and scones were of a high order and soon we had families making a weekly pilgrimage to enjoy our teas!

To help things along, I boarded a few dogs, trimmed a few others, bred the odd litter, bought and sold puppies, and added to my farming activities in the guise of 'small stock'. In less than no time I had a flourishing rabbitry, adding guinea pigs and fancy mice, all breeding at a rate of knots and eminently saleable. In her spare time mother made all the hutches and the mouse house, using her considerable skill for carpentry to turn those wonderful Tate and Lyle sugar boxes and the smaller margarine boxes, all made in good wood, into suitable homes for my stock. While the garage housed the rabbits and cavies, the shed was the mouse house and the glass-fronted cages were soon stacked from floor to ceiling. Mice breed at a great rate and have enormous families. A pair of mice can have several thousand descendants in just one year!

The young mice were counted and boxed up and despatched to various pet shops around the country. This sounds easy until *you* have to do the boxing up. Small mice are like quicksilver and can leap out of the hand and jump enormous distances. Catching, counting and holding on to these little creatures requires quite a degree of experience and expertise, you also have to like mice—which I do. They have very sharp little teeth which they do not hesitate to use on the unwary finger, and if you catch them by the tail, except at the root, they shed it, leaving you with the pink strand in your hand while the erstwhile owner skips off to a new lifestyle to re-grow his

41

nether appendage. More time was spent catching, counting and boxing mice than I care to remember.

I started with a pair of white mice given me by
my stepsister, but both turned out to be males, and I
made the mistake of getting wives for them which is
how the mouse industry started. Later I added coloured
mice which fetched higher prices, and as mice of all
colours made their escape into the wild on various occasions, I often wondered what the next inhabitants of the
bungalow would think when they found the place infested by piebald and multi-coloured rodents! The guinea
pigs multiplied at a slower though pretty deliberate rate
but did not produce as many young in a litter as the mice,
and were always well in demand as pets. I have a copy of
advertisements I ran in the local paper: 'Auntie! Have you
forgotten those white mice for Johnny?', 'Grandpa! Buy
Betty a bunny for her birthday!' and sundry similar ads.
Always a great one for advertisement if it meant an
increase in trade, I contacted the local press when one of
the white mice started making strange musical noises, and
several papers ran stories of the 'singing mouse' which
helped to get my enterprise before the public gaze. I think
the mouse probably had a touch of bronchitis, but you
would hardly have got one of those old-type country vets
to take you seriously if you suggested such a thing!

My mother decided to breed budgerigars after being
given a pair by a neighbour who moved away. Her
London-based sister, who had their father's taste for exotic
animals, had kept a small monkey that turned savage and
was presented to London Zoo, though what this august

body had done to deserve the unpleasant creature is anyone's guess. The wooden cage in which the monkey had resided being vacant, my mother asked if she could borrow it for conversion to an outdoor aviary, a request to which my aunt readily acceded. Aunt and two cousins duly arrived in their large, old car complete with bedding to stay overnight. They also brought the monkey cage and a full complement of white Pekinese which my aunt was breeding at the time. The bedding for their overnight stay was needed, as by then mother had realised the potential of bed and breakfast, and our bedroom and the small spare room were full of overnight guests. Mother slept on the sitting room sofa, and I rolled up in blankets on the floor, joined by aunt and cousins who thought the whole thing an enormous joke, and brought packets of bacon and pounds of sausages which they cooked up and consumed with great gusto.

The outdoor aviary was put up that weekend. It looked good, roofed with weatherproof felting, and the budgies in their cage were brought out to be ceremoniously transferred to their breeding apartments. Sadly, the door through which the monkey had come and gone was quite large, and instead of nailing it up and making a small aperture the family endeavoured to transfer the birds from cage to cage through a fairly large opening. The inevitable happened: during transfer the birds sensed freedom, doubled back through the wide opening as soon as free of the restraining hand, and made their escape into the opposite wood never to be seen again—mother's cage-bird breeding programme came to a grinding halt.

Rabbits, of course, have their own laws, and certainly reproduce quickly if not restrained. However, in my case, I restricted their desires to the required litters from the best sellers: this meant colour, which at the time was white rabbits with pink eyes. In later years my rabbitries (I had several) contained the popular brown Havana, the Silver Fox and the exotic Rex varieties.

My love for horses was unabated, but riding lessons were out of the question. There was no money for such things. However, the local butcher's vans were still horse-drawn, and in his field behind the shop he had a rare collection of equines. On one of my visits to purchase the dogs' meat, which consisted of sheep's head, offcuts and breasts of lamb, I enquired casually about the horses and ponies he kept. The butcher was proud of his transport, many of the animals were Welsh cobs straight from the valleys, and very flashy they were too as they careered about the countryside on the rounds. 'Does anyone ride them?' I asked casually. 'Well, not really,' was the reply, 'but if you want a ride there is a bridle and saddle in the shed, help yourself if you can catch one.' Magic words to my ears. Of course the punch line should have been heeded—'if you can catch one.'

The very next day I was down in the field with a rope halter found in the shed. There were some ten animals in the field all peacefully grazing, but as soon as I approached them they raised their heads, turned to one another, said something amusing and all high-tailed it to the other side of the field where they stood defiantly under an oak tree, snorting ruderies at me. Previous to this my sole experience with horses had been with the big farm variety, quiet in all gears as they say. I had learned to groom them, to know where and when they wore a certain harness, and to keep my feet well away from theirs. I had also learned to sit on their broad backs as they patiently plodded home tired from a day's work. Apart from that and a few jollies on seaside donkeys, I was, as they say, pig-ignorant, or should that be horse-ignorant? However, I had my mother's determination and once set on a project would not give up until I had accomplished what I set out to do.

I had acquired from the local jumble sale a pair of ill-fitting cotton-cord riding breeches which were my pride and joy, and these worn with rubber boots (not known as wellies then) and a check shirt, were my riding costume; hats did not come into it. It took me a week, going each day, to catch one of the cobs, a fairly friendly mare who succumbed eventually to a pocketful of carrots and allowed me to slip the halter over her ears and lead her to the fence by the shed where I tied her up. The other nine accompanied us at a respectful distance, nudging each other and giving their companion enquiring looks. In the shed I found a very small saddle with incredibly fine metal stirrups on narrow leathers, and a bridle consisting of cheekpieces, a headband, a very light snaffle bit and one pair of rather frayed reins. It was not until long after that I discovered this was the tack used by the butcher's young nephew when he took a pony to one of the illegal 'flapping' meetings held on summer evenings at a secret rendezvous. To my untutored mind this situation was glorious: a saddle and bridle and a horse *at last*! The mare stood quietly as I did up the girth and put the bridle on. With a thumping heart I climbed up into the little saddle and all hell broke loose.

With one bound the mare set off at a flat gallop across the field accompanied by all her friends, who bucked and kicked in a frenzy of delight at this novel way of breaking the boredom of perpetual grazing. How I clung on I do not know, perhaps my experience in the past with Duchess helped, but it was not until the mare came to an abrupt stop at the ditch in front of the hedge at the far end of the field, that I shot over her head to land in a bramble bush. It then took an hour to catch her again and remount, only to have the same thing happen once more—some idiots never learn.

Still persevering, I told mother nothing of my experiences. Saying I was out looking at likely stock to buy for resale, each day I sneaked off to the butcher's field. By the end of the second week the mare came to greet me, eager for the carrots, and let me tack her up and mount her; we even negotiated a sedate walk round the field at the beginning of the third week, but once her companions decided on a bit of fun, off we all went and I ended up as usual in the ditch. How long this would have gone on, and whether I would have eventually mastered the situation, is anyone's guess, but you cannot keep anything secret in a small village and some busybody told my mother, with great glee, what I was up to. In a trice my riding career came to an abrupt end for the foreseeable future.

One day a notice appeared in the window of the Post

Office: 'For Sale. St Bernard dog. 50/-.' Fifty shillings was two pounds fifty, not a lot in this day and age but quite an amount then and equal to the weekly wage of some men. However, sensing a bargain, I hurried round to the address given; a big old house on the edge of the village. The vendor was the housekeeper who had been left the dog in the will of her lately deceased employer. She did not like dogs, could not think why he kept such a dog, and wanted rid of it as soon as possible. After a bit of haggling I paid 45 shillings for Pickles, his collar and lead, feeding bowl and pedigree. He was one of the most charming dogs I have ever owned. It was apparent that the woman had not bothered with him after his master died as he was painfully thin. He was pathetically grateful for anything offered to him, and immediately attached himself to my side, taking readily to his new name of Bruce (well, you could not call a dog as big as this one—and he was a giant—Pickles, could you?) He even took to sleeping under my bed, and when he got up to turn round in the night the whole bed heaved up in the air. This was all right until some bed and breakfasters came to stay; the couple in mother's room and the old granny in mine. I was busy spreading out the bedding on the sitting room floor when I heard a shriek from my bedroom, and rushed in. Bruce was just composing himself for the night and had not yet lain down so the bed plus its rather frail occupant were balanced on his broad back! The old lady's relatives rushed in, failed to see the funny side; dressed, packed and left without paying for their supper.

At the time of Bruce taking up residence, my mother got acquainted with Mr Cooper, a disreputable old smallholder who sold vegetables and fruit at reasonable prices. He called twice weekly, bringing his produce in a rickety old trap drawn by an ancient black pony mare. It was not long before I had inveigled the old chap into letting me drive the pony, and I got on fine up and down the road, but unfortunately I did not gauge the turn into our gate quite accurately and hit the gatepost an almighty crack, which split it in half and took the wheel off the trap. The ensuing bills set us back on necessities for several weeks. Mr Cooper, having been suitably reimbursed for the damage caused to his ancient equipage, gave me some driving lessons. I got quite proficient and this stood me in good stead a few years later.

Bruce did not care for our new-found friend, who looked like an unwashed scarecrow in his raggedy clothes, old cap pulled over his red, whiskered face, and growly laugh when he showed a mouthful of broken, blackened teeth. Mother and I were both out one day when he called with the vegetables—an unusual occurrence. I was down the road looking for 'Peter Rabbit', the white Angora buck, who had an annoying habit of unlatching his cage and going walkabout. He was quite well known in the village, and various children had earned pennies returning him to base. As I came through the gate, clasping the escapee to my bosom, I saw Mr Cooper's pony and trap parked on the gravel, and then I realised that he was pressed flat against the garage wall, with Bruce, long trails of saliva hanging from his pendulous lips, standing on his hind legs, a giant front paw either side of the terrified man's head, peering enquiringly into the whiskery face. I burst out laughing and called the dog off; sadly Mr Cooper did not think it at all funny, and from that day on our produce was left at the front gate, Mr C resolutely refusing ever to enter the premises again.

Bruce was a mighty eater: firstly he had to be fattened up from his emaciated state, and then he had to be kept in good fettle—it all cost too much for our slender resources and so sadly, the big dog had to be sold. He was fortunate, for a butcher in a nearby small town was looking for a dog to give would-be intruders pause for thought, and yet be a pet for his children. Bruce was ideal: gentle and kind, he loved children and settled happily in his new home, allowing the babies to ride on his back, the older children to attach him to a little cart or dress him up in odd costumes, and thriving on all the wonderful food provided by his new owner. I wept a few tears at his departure, for no one could fail to love him, but the six pounds that the new owner paid helped a great deal towards our expenses.

At this time the then Duchess of York bought the first Pembroke Corgi for the Princesses Elizabeth and Margaret. Many connected with dogs reckoned that the new royal pet would be greatly in demand nationally, and in this they proved correct. I bought a bitch of the breed through an advertisement in *Our Dogs*. She came straight from a farm in Wales, and continued her work of rounding up and nipping heels when she arrived. After she had displayed her skill on several tradespeople my mother

49

issued an edict—she had to go—so she went, to a local farmer who said she was the best herder he had ever had; his milking herd did not know what had hit them! The next corgi came as a puppy, also from Wales. She was a dear little soul but seemed to have a strange, fluffy coat. As she got older it was painfully apparent that one of her parents had had more than a nodding acquaintance with a Pomeranian, and I sold her as a pet to a widow, and the two got on famously.

As corgis were obviously not for me, I accepted one of my favourites as a gift from a local breeder, a blue roan cocker spaniel. This was a two year old bitch and I was to breed from her and the former owners the Oldhams would have a couple of pups back. They were as impecunious as we were, and we all got on famously. They had a large kennel of cockers, around 40 dogs and bitches, but not nearly enough capital to keep them, and were always on the breadline. However, they both had an enormous sense of humour and bore their troubles with cheerful fortitude, and kept going on copious draughts of strong tea and innumerable packets of cigarettes. They often said that their idea of hell was a place where the fire was so hot you could not get near enough to put the kettle on or light your cigarette! My mother was of the opinion that they only bought food for the dogs, seldom for themselves, and frequently invited them to eat with us, being quite sure it was the only proper meal they ever had.

The Oldhams were very experienced breeders and taught me a great deal; we spent many a night sitting up with whelping bitches and seeing umpteen litters into the world, and they also taught me how to dock the tiny puppies safely and cleanly and without hurt. Sadly their kennel had an outbreak of mange; they had thought that some of the adults were clear, including my bitch, but she soon showed symptoms and went back to her former owners. I was deprived not only of a brood bitch but also of my first show dog for another year.

Two fox terriers and two Scotties joined the family and like all terriers they were full of devilry. The Scotties, at six months of age, bit a hole in the wire of their run and got out into the neighbour's garden where they killed six of his point-of-lay pullets which we had to pay for. When the little horrors did this for a second time they were hastily sold.

Around that time I had a bit of a crush on a man called Norman. He acted as combined station-master, porter, ticket collector and general dogsbody at our local 'halt', and I got to know him when sending off the endless boxes of small stock by train to the various purchasers. He was a nice man, some 15 years my senior. He owned a delightful black Labrador called Paddy, who took a tremendous fancy to me, although, at the time, I think I would rather have had his owner's affections!

Norman was a frequent visitor to our bungalow, coming for meals as he lived alone in a bedsitter, and my mother was, of course, sorry for him. Norman came in useful to lend a hand fetching straw and hay for our stock as he had a four-seater square-set car with little grey tasselled blinds at the windows, and we rattled happily all round the narrow Hampshire lanes. Norman used to laugh and say: 'What would we do if we met a Rolls Royce?' It was a standing joke—but one day we did and found out, the chauffeur of the imposing car making Norman reverse his contraption a quarter of a mile and pull in at a farm gate!

Paddy was always with Norman, but one day he decided he wanted to stay with us. Norman took him home but by evening Paddy was back on our doorstep. Norman fetched him home. The same thing happened next day and continued for some weeks, but by then our time in the village was running out. Perhaps the local shopkeepers decided we owed them too much; anyway things were going from bad to worse. We sold all the stock, paid the bills, and packed our belongings. Norman and Paddy saw us off at the little station, and the last sight I had was of the black dog sitting looking terribly forlorn—one of my old slippers dangling from his mouth.

CHAPTER SIX

At eleven o'clock on the morning of September 3rd 1939 I was sitting in the back of an old green van surrounded by luggage and hanging on to the leads of around 12 assorted dogs. It was not the conventional way for anyone to start serving their country at the outbreak of a world war. Briefly, the events leading up to this situation were these. After Hampshire my mother and I went to live in a maisonette in Maida Vale, I think to be near her sister. This did not suit me greatly so I went back off to the country and worked for several kennels, eventually coming to the London home to work a month for an old butcher of a veterinary surgeon. I could not stand his methods, so left and started a small boarding kennel and trimming business at our maisonette, and by then had a few cockers of my own which I exhibited with scant success.

In those days there were several big dog shows held in London, and most of the people coming up from the country travelled by train and did not know their way across London. One of my 'services' was to meet people and get them and their dogs safely to and from the venue—it helped pay the bills. That was how I got to know Mr and Mrs W who bred gundogs. A farmer and

53

his wife from Somerset they were grateful for my help, and as rumours of war to come were in the air, asked me what I intended to do should a conflict take place. I said I would join the Women's Land Army, and enthusiastically they invited me down to their farm to work for them. I was quite thrilled about this and accepted the offer, never thinking that war was actually on the way; however, it was, and as the realisation sank in mother and I made ready to leave London for the farm. Mother arranged for our furniture to go in store, and I responded to some of my customers' pleas to take their precious pets with me and board them until it was safe for them to return. The promise of weekly payment was too strong to resist, and I accepted nine dogs, which with my own and mother's Yorkies, who travelled in their baskets, made a full complement for the van. The newest puppy was accommodated in a box balanced on mother's knees.

Our chauffeur was an old, grumpy man with un-trimmed moustache and an obvious dislike for his elderly vehicle by the way he wrenched at the wheel and swore at it. As we drove off, precisely at eleven o'clock, the sirens sounded, and a number of people ran screaming down the pavement; for what reason I am not sure. At each crossing there was a policeman clad in full gear: gas cape, respirator etc. It was all quite macabre and we were glad to leave London behind. The van proceeded at around 35 miles per hour—well, it was old and heavily loaded. We had two stops for the dogs and one to eat the packets of sandwiches my mother had provided.

It was around five o'clock when we reached the village

which was our destination. Bathed in warm autumn sunshine the old cottages looked charming, the gardens full of bright-coloured dahlias, and apple trees laden with rosy-cheeked fruit. An elderly man indicated the lane we required and cast a quizzical glance at us when we asked where the farm was located. 'Oh, them!' he growled in a strange manner. 'Mile down, 'tis on your left.' We turned into a very narrow lane, with high banks on each side, winding down for a mile. Ahead of us and bathed in sun was a beautiful old house with a large hole in the roof. 'What a pity that lovely place has been allowed to fall into ruins,' said my mother. 'I hate to tell you,' I replied, peering through the grill in the back wall of the van and looking over her shoulder at the sign which hung from one nail at the gate, 'but that is the farm!' There was what can only be described as a pregnant pause, as our driver grunted and swung the van through the opening, the gate being off its hinges in the ditch.

We drove into a deserted farmyard surrounded by huge old barns all of which were in the same sad state of decay as the house. There was no sign of life, and the old man got out and hammered on the back door. It was some moments before it opened and Mrs W appeared. She looked at us with wonder as if we had come from Mars. My mother was by now out of the van. 'Well, here we are at last,' she exclaimed brightly, and then seeing the woman's look, 'you *were* expecting us?' 'Oh, er, yes, come in.' Mrs W turned to go in. 'But where are the kennels for the dogs?' asked my mother. 'We must get them settled first.' When we had made final arrangements the W's had offered kenneling for all I could bring. Mrs W did not answer but shouted shrilly for her husband, who came shambling out.

This was not the neatly dressed country couple I had shepherded across the Metropolis on several occasions— here were two dingy slatterns. Mrs W's hair was straggling down from a few ill-placed hair pins. She had on a dirty blouse and worn skirt and old plimsoles with the toes out. He was in stained breeches and gaiters, along with a torn flannel shirt, and displayed several days growth of beard. They seemed less than pleased to see us. 'The kennels,' insisted my mother. Mr W opened the back door of the van, surveyed the occupants in their cramped conditions, and jerked his head sideways. 'Best bring 'em on.' He started towards the rear of the house. There were, of course, no kennels. I was offered a crumbling old cottage with glassless windows and a stone floor. Mr W told me I could hammer some staples in the walls and tie the dogs up there. He brought a few armfuls of straw and I bedded the animals down as well as I could, fed and watered them and went in to see how my mother was getting on. She was sitting at the large table in the old stone-flagged kitchen looking rather down and sipping strong black tea from a chipped willow pattern cup. A huge open fire took up the whole of one wall, and a black pot on a ratchet hung over the flames; something with a strange odour was bubbling within. Beside the open hearth a bread oven was set in the wall. No sink, the only water was from a pump in the yard.

After our cup of tea Mrs W indicated that she would

show us our rooms. We had been allotted the small parlour, and the case of stuffed birds, and the antimacassars took me right back to my childhood and Uncle Henry's farm; sadly, that is where the resemblance ended. We were then conducted up the wide, curved oak stairs that terminated on a landing directly under a hole in the roof. When one looked up it was to observe the ceiling stained and sagging, and on the floor several pails were placed to catch the drips when it rained. Our bedroom faced towards the front and was big enough for a dance hall. It contained a large wardrobe, a chest of drawers, a wash-hand stand with china fittings, a chair with a broken cane seat, and one worn rag rug placed between the two single iron bedsteads.

'Where is the bathroom?' asked Mother. 'Bathroom!' exclaimed Mrs W. 'We don't have none of that, lavatory is down here.' We followed her down the passage to a door which she flung open to display a large mahogany seat; when you looked down the aperture it was to see that all offerings ended in a pit below the house. It was not a place to drop your wedding ring or your false teeth. My mother stood in shocked silence. 'How is it emptied?' she enquired. 'Emptied? Well, I don't rightly know, we'm only bin 'ere 20 years so it ain't bin necessary!' There was no more to be said on that theme, so we retired to our bedroom where our bags had been left. When the door closed mother sank wearily on to the bed and then froze. 'Dear,' she said in an icy tone, 'this mattress is stuffed with straw!'

My mother never went anywhere without her own

bed linen, and so we made up the spartan beds as best we might. After a supper of bread and cheese and pickles, we lighted our candles and went upstairs; undressing wearily we climbed into bed and snuffed out the lights. We had not been lying there more than 20 minutes when my mother asked, 'Are you itching?' I replied that, yes I was. We lighted the candles, and getting out flung back the clothes. The beds were alive with fleas!

In the morning my mother, tired and cross after a night wrapped in a blanket and sleeping on the chair, told our hostess about the fleas. 'Oh, we 'ave 'em too, but we don't take no notice' was the careless answer as she spread the fat bacon and bread and jam out for breakfast. By then I had seen to the dogs as best I could, but had already decided that all the 'boarders' would have to be returned to their owners, and this was done during the coming week, leaving only my own dogs to be seen to, my mother's little Yorkies being in the house with us.

I was expected to report for milking the first morning although I had not officially joined the WLA. Out I went, in the same old cotton-cord breeches that had seen my debut as a rider! The cowshed roof had long fallen in, and the herd of some 30 Shorthorns were crowded into a small, iron-railed yard. They were very placid which was fortunate as one had to push amongst them with bucket and stool, and squash underneath to do the milking. They seemed quite used to the exercise and all stood around cudding while we accomplished the task. The dairy was dusty and when I asked about a cooler I was informed that they didn't use one; neither was there a strainer, the milk was just tipped into the churns and the milk lorry would collect it at nine o'clock or thereabouts. The milk was marvellous: overnight the cream set inches thick on top, and every morning Mrs W scooped two jugfuls off for house use.

Mother determined to go to the village and buy some Keatings Powder to kill the fleas, and old Joe, who did odd jobs on the farm, offered her a lift in the 'putt'; this was a two-wheeled farm cart used for carrying roots and muck spreading and was drawn by Betty the farm work-horse. My mother, who was always correctly dressed, sat on a sack in the putt; she wore a hat, her gloves and carried her handbag and shopping basket. The Keatings certainly cleared out the fleas, but they had indelibly left their marks on the beautiful linen sheets which had been a gift from my grandmother.

Although I worked on the farm my mother had to pay for our board and lodging, and this was a bit of a problem as sending the dogs back and feeding our own had used up most of our slender resources. I asked how I set about joining the Women's Land Army, and after nagging a bit, got Mr W to send a message via Joe and through various village folk to the 'big house', wherein resided the Hon. Mrs B who was enrolling the girls for land work. The Hon. Mrs B arrived in an ancient, chauffeur-driven Daimler: a kind, elderly lady, willing and keen, but with little knowledge of the job in hand about which she appeared to be very poorly briefed. She took my name and said she would put me on her list, but as I already had land work, she would not be contacting me any more.

There were no uniforms available so early in the conflict, but I should no doubt get some clothes at a later date— good job I still had the cord breeches. Of course the old dear should have given me a number, but she signally failed to do this, and it was not discovered until I had been 18 months in the WLA. They resolutely refused to backdate my service to the start of hostilities, which meant I was credited with 18 months less service than I had done, and did not qualify for all the scarlet half-diamond bits of cloth we were sent to be sewn on our greatcoat sleeves to signify each six months of service. I was always three short—a fact that rankles to this day.

For the first ten days things proceeded fairly smoothly. I helped with the milking, swept the cow yard, fed calves and bagged up the windfalls in the orchard. One evening we loaded all the bags of apples into the putt, and Mr W invited me to join him for a trip to a local farmer friend who made his own cider. It was quite a large farm but the yards were deep in manure and many of the buildings needed patching. The only clean shed was that alloted to the farmer's youngest daughter Cissie for her 'Young Farmers calf'; the YFC had a calf scheme in those days for the best calf reared by a member. Cissie's Young Farmers calf stood up to its belly in deep golden straw and was obviously groomed on a daily basis; very different to the calves in the next pen who were hock-deep in muck and had cleats of manure clinging to their tails and hindquarters.

We backed the putt into the big double doors of a large, dim barn where the cider mill and press were situated. I climbed a ladder and looked down on the mill, which was covered in thick dust, old straw and dead rats and birds. Our bags of apples were hauled out and tipped carelessly on top of all this. I asked Mr W on the drive home why the farmer had not cleaned the mill before tipping in the apples, he replied that it was unnecessary, a bit of muck gave the cider a rare taste!

Another evening was spent rabbit shooting: I nearly got my head blown off as Mr W swung his 12-bore round on a bolting bunny and I only just ducked in time. He swore roundly at me and said it was my fault.

The farmer's show dogs were housed in one of the decaying barns, living as a pack of about 10 on filthy straw that was never changed. Every week or ten days, as time allowed, old Joe drove the putt to the slaughter house bringing back a load of paunches, bullocks' heads and bones, and on arrival pulled the pin out and tipped the whole mass into the dirty yard. This was the dogs' food, and they were let out to grab and cart back to their barn any tasty morsel they fancied, grinding up bones and chewing the unwashed and slimy green paunches with loud growls. As the summer of 1939 was a warm one, the leftovers soon became covered in bluebottles, and in a short time the eggs they laid turned into a heaving mass of maggots which did not put the dogs off in the least. When thirsty the dogs, standing on their hind legs, lapped from the horse trough. You would think dogs kept like this would suffer from dire complaints but I have never seen a healthier lot in my life! All, however, were not so lucky: it was two weeks after my arrival that I found Beauty, a blue,

61

roan and tan bitch of the old, and then, scarce Field spaniel breed, a poor emaciated soul suckling a litter of 10 puppies. Mr W had taken a dislike to her and did not feed her; she had only what she could scavenge. We had a blazing row and he gave her to me on the spot, if I cared to feed her, but he wanted all the puppies. This arrangement was carried out, and when we left the farm Beauty came with us; alas, she was too undernourished and suffering too badly with skin problems to be saved, and I had to have her put to sleep. However, she was, for me, the start of a lifetime in the Field spaniel breed.

Mr W had a riding horse, an ancient ex point-to-pointer called Lofty. He was a lean, sad animal; we struck up an immediate friendship, and Mr W told me I could ride him when my work was done. So in the evenings I saddled up and climbed aboard and went off round the fields where Lofty taught me how to stay on at all paces, even if it was with no style. However, it was eventually Lofty who was to cause our hurried exit from the farm.

We had not been at the farm two weeks when we discovered two things: Mr W was a drunk and his wife an epileptic. We discovered the latter first when we came into the kitchen to find Mrs W wandering about in a dazed condition with ash all over her face and clothes. My mother tackled Mr W who admitted that his wife did fall about a bit, but that it 'wer'nt nothing' and none of our business anyway. The fact that Mr W was a lush became only too obvious when he rolled home at night belligerent and shouting. We could hear him from our room and stayed put with the door locked.

At the end of the fifth week the crunch came. Mr W sometimes rode Lofty up to the pub at lunchtime and then galloped him home, rolling in the saddle in a drunken daze. One afternoon when man and horse had been missing for several hours, I was just going to get the cows in for milking when I heard the wildly clattering hoofs of the old horse on the lane. As he galloped into the yard Lofty was reined in with a wild jagging at the bit, his rider falling off with a grunt. Blood was running from Lofty's mouth and from rips in his sides where the spurs Mr W was wearing had torn his hide. Flying into a blind fury and shouting at the rider as he fell off, I grabbed the reins and choking with anger led the horse into the stable to attend to his wounds. But I was unlucky, as I slipped the bridle off and tied Lofty up, Mr W lurched in and made a lunge for me, shouting in obscene terms what he intended to do when he laid hands on me. Quick as a flash I bobbed under the horse's belly and out the other side making for the door. The drunken and enraged farmer picked up the pitchfork and began to chase me. I made the house yards ahead, and jumping through the kitchen door snatched the hunting whip from its nail on the wall, and stood my ground. Cursing and swearing Mr W stumbled through the door and made for me. As he came forward I swung the whip and caught him a full blow across the cheek. Dropping the whip I ran for our parlour where mother was sewing, slammed and locked the door. The time had come for our departure.

Mr W was silent and morose the next day. I did the milking and kept a wary eye on his every move, but he

63

neither spoke nor even looked in my direction. Mother got Joe to take her to the village where she caught the bus to Taunton, returning in the evening to say that she had rented a small cottage that had three acres of land and orchard, for ten shillings a week, and we were to move in three days. She had also contacted the store in London that housed our furniture and it would arrive when we did.

We moved on a Wednesday using a local farmer's waggon and two horses to transport us the eight or so miles to our new abode. Mother sat up by the driver; she was wearing her best hat and white gloves and clutching her handbag. In the body of the wagon I sat surrounded by our luggage and the baskets of Yorkies, holding on to the spaniels' leads. It was with a sigh of pure relief that we arrived at the gate of the tiny cottage in the remote village—we may have been penniless and jobless but at least we were safe. And so the next phase of my farming career began.

CHAPTER SEVEN

If the farm had been infested with fleas, the cottage proved to be infested with mice. The first night that we snuggled gratefully into our own bed in the one tiny bedroom, we were awakened by a movement across the eiderdown, and lighting the candle we were in time to see around half a dozen mice using the obstruction as a highway. We were, however, far too tired to care, and blowing out the candle were soon asleep. Despite mousetraps and a cat we never did get rid of the mice, who continued to share our bedroom for all the time we were there. Mother's favourite treat, when finances would allow, was Fry's Chocolate Cream, which she ate in bed, and her habit of leaving part of a bar for the next night no doubt gave the mice the idea that not only was a bed being provided but breakfast as well.

Apart from our bedroom, there was a tiny landing and a sitting room with a 'kitchener'—that is a black stove used for cooking, and fed with coal or wood: a temperamental beast at the mercy of the wind and its own foul nature. The front door opened directly into the sitting room; the stairs were on the right and a door in the rear wall led to the scullery which was narrow and ran the length of the cottage. The scullery was high, no ceiling, just the roof beams, and contained a copper; there was no sink, but mains water was supplied by a tap in the yard.

The scullery had a door either end, one leading to the yard and one to the garden that ran alongside the road. The lavatory was, of course, an earth closet housed in a sentry box, next to the pigsty, beyond the granary in the yard. The bucket had to be emptied at least twice a week, and mother and I used to wait until nearly dark to stagger with the load across the yard, through the scullery and out into the garden where I had previously dug a hole. This had been the custom of generations of former inhabitants and the garden was the best manured and had the finest soil and grew the best vegetables I have ever seen! Mother was frightfully shy about this 'night soil' business, and if there was a sign of anyone, even in the distance, we had to wait, poised inside the garden door with the bucket, until she gave the signal to move.

Mother always insisted on a hot bath before she dressed each day. When she could not get a proper bath she made do in a basin, as at the farm. Things were better now. Each morning after she had got the kitchener going she boiled up two buckets of water, and when they were ready, we brought in a tin bath and mother proceeded with her ablutions on the mat in front of the fire, after which I followed her in. Then the bath containing the soapy water had to be carefully carried outside and emptied. It was time-consuming but at least it showed that we had not, as mother put it, 'let ourselves go.'

There was quite a good bit of garden on one side of the cottage, and on the other a yard with a six stall cowshed, a cart shed, two pigsties and the granary. The latter was a good, solid, stone building, and came complete with two inhabitants: a pair of pigeons, one pink and one blue, which we christened Lucy and Basil. These two furnished us with many a good meal, as they spent their lives perched on the beam billing and cooing, copulating frequently, and laying eggs, which were incubated with great diligence in their makeshift nest. As soon as the squabs were out of the nest and big and fat enough, I used to climb the ladder in the half-light and remove them, and roast pigeon or pie was on the menu. This sent the original pair into another flurry of lovemaking and nest arranging and the whole process was repeated.

The land attached to the cottage consisted of a large field and a long, narrow orchard with some forty-two trees mostly of cider apples but with the odd 'Tom Putt', an old Somersetshire apple of great size and with a rosy face, soft and sweet to eat but not a keeper. Many of the trees were heavy with growths of mistlestoe. It was a blessing to move in when the orchard was full; Old Garge, who lived nearby, bought all the crop and I helped him pick and bag them.

Old Garge was a member of a family named Dark; he had seven brothers and all of them farmed small acreages in and around the village. Old Garge had twenty-two acres at the bottom of the hill. He was a widower and lived with his ne'er-do-well son Tony, who was supposed to help his father but did as little as possible. Jim Dark, the brother next in age, farmed just up the road from us. He had fifty acres and a family of eight. Old Garge was a wonderful character: a little, lean, gnarled man with a bright red face and twinkling blue eyes under bushy brows. He wore the countryman's uniform of worn cord trousers tied below the knee, hobnailed boots, a sagging jacket and greasy cap, and in winter a discarded army greatcoat that reached to his heels, and from the rear caused him to resemble pictures of the retreat from Moscow.

Old Garge had three cows of incredible antiquity: May, Daisy and Belle. He had been grazing these in our field, keeping the grass down while the place was unoccupied, and offered my mother two shillings a week each for the grazing and this satisfactory offer was accepted. Unlike most farmers, Old Garge did not have regular milking hours. His red face had not been arrived at by good fresh air alone: he made and drank his own cider, and was so puggled some evenings that he arrived around eleven o'clock, weaving his way up the field with stool, pail and lantern, to crouch under May, Daisy and Belle in all weathers; abstracting, not without difficulty, the pitiful amount of milk the three produced from their stringy bags. Morning milking was the same: he could arrive at six with the lark, or as late as noon, but as the milk yield was so poor, and he only used it for his own consumption, it did not matter much. We offered him the loan of the cowshed where he could milk in comfort, but he declined saying, 'Fresh air never hurt no one.' But he agreed to leave the stool in there hanging on the wall.

Old Garge had two modes of transport. One was a rusty bicycle with no brakes, so that when he went back

down the hill, milk pail hanging from one handlebar, he
had to trail one booted foot on the rough road to stop
himself hurtling down and finishing in the duck pond on
the bend at the foot of the hill. His second means of
getting around was old Dolly and a putt. Dolly and her
master were of the same vintage and the two old things
were a familiar sight in the neighbourhood. Dolly was a
bay with an unkempt mane and a docked tail with a few
strands of black hair that wisped at the flies. She was gaunt
and bony but still strong, though her lacklustre eyes
seemed world-weary. Dolly was soon taken under my
wing. The free grazing offered was readily accepted, and
she filled out just a bit. In return I was able to ride her
bareback to the village to collect the groceries.

Luscious blackberries hung on the hedge that divided
our paddock from the next-door field. 'You can sell they
to the blackberry man,' advised old Garge knowingly.
Twice a week the blackberry man with his horse and cart
called, paying a good price, all the berries being sent north
to make dye for sailors' uniforms. The blackberries, and
mushrooms filched from a nearby field at first light, were
sold for a shilling a pound at the gate and brought in
enough to pay for necessities.

I wrote to the Hon. Mrs B, giving our new address, and
she passed my name to a lady of the same ilk who called
and told me sourly that I was unlikely to get a farm job
round there as the farmers' wives were suspicious of
the Land Girls and thought they had just joined up to
steal their husbands! She also said the uniforms were on
their way. Sure enough a large parcel bearing an official

stamp arrived. Tearing it open I found a pair of velvet cord breeches. 'Try them on,' urged my mother looking worried. It was as well I did, for they had obviously been made for a woman of twenty stone and the crutch came level with my knees. So back they went.

Over the next few months the uniform arrived in dribs and drabs: first another pair of breeches that almost fitted, then two buff-coloured Aertex shirts with short sleeves, a green woollen pullover, khaki dungarees, long hose and a pair of hobnailed walking shoes, that gave me hell at first, but which proved most comfortable and suitable foot-wear once they and my feet had got used to one another. Lastly came the wonderful overcoat, in the manner of an army officer's greatcoat, and a felt hat with a wide brim, and with these a gas cape, all that was on offer for wet weather, which tore horribly on every thorn and jagged object. Much later we had a trench coat-type mackintosh which did not keep out any rain, not even a light shower. I never wore all the uniform at once, only in bits, as I always believed in being individual.

It was imperative to find work and I answered an advertisement in the local paper for 'A temporary part-time rider to work in a horse dealer's yard.' The yard was situated just outside Taunton. Strangely enough, in spite of my inexperience, I got the job but had no way of getting in to the stables as the bus only went to and from the village three days a week. So Mr Drew, the dealer lent me Joey.

Joey was a 15 hands part Welsh cob of a dirty-brown colour. He was a charming and useful sort, without a nasty thought in his head, and he was equally handy under saddle or between the shafts. I was also lent a saddle and bridle, and rode the eight miles to work in the early light, and back home in the evening, and each day I worked I was paid five shillings. Joey spent his nights in the field with the three old cows and they became great chums. He was, however, a bit of a nuisance when old Garge came to milk, as he always imagined the pail contained oats or some such and would poke his big head over Garge's shoulder, and once tipped the old boy off the stool. On days when I did not have to go to work and we were picking the blackberries Joey accompanied us, and if not given a handful of fruit at intervals, he pushed us gently in the back with his soft nose, causing us to end up in the ditch with berries spilled, whereupon he joined us and demolished the lot.

My duties at the yard included mucking out and tack cleaning, but mostly climbing up on any and every quadruped Mr Drew bought to 'see what they did'. If I could manage to stay on for several circuits of the ash track, the animal was sold as a lady's hunter! I had a number of crashing falls, but never got hurt. There was a skewbald stallion in one box who had been bought from a circus, and all sorts of noises and sights caused him to stand up on his hind legs, which made him pretty unsaleable. I used to be sent off round the town on this beast to 'get him used to things.' He stood up at white lines on roads, at the sound of bells or whistles, and if a car honked a horn. I had some pretty adventurous rides but never came off, and he taught me a lot about staying aboard.

Another day Mr Drew harnessed Joey to the dogcart and we drove from Taunton to Chard where he had some grazing land. The idea was to bring back two mares and some youngsters of two and three years of age. When we drove back I led the mares on halters over the back of the dogcart and the four or five assorted youngsters followed the mares in loose formation, kept more or less together by the attentions of Mr Drew's lurcher. The job was temporary because the position was usually filled by Mr Drew's niece, who had taken time off to get married, and she soon came back and I was out of work again.

Through the local postmistress who, like all of her ilk in those days, was a mine of information and gossip, I heard that the owner of the 'big house' was looking for someone to work with his poultry. He was a good-looking and charming man in his thirties, one of the partners in an old firm of estate agents, of which his father had been senior partner until his premature death in the mid 1920s. Much village mythology surrounded this man whose young wife had tragically died leaving him with a baby daughter. The stories about the event were many and varied, and the tale of his heartbroken life was the currency over many a teapot. It was told that at midnight he was to be seen praying at his wife's grave on which he left a single red rose. So intrigued was I with this romantic story that one night I walked the mile to the church, hid in the shrubs and watched for this pathetic scene to take place. I had a wasted journey: no one arrived and as far as I could see there had been no flowers on the grave for quite some time. So when I heard that there was actually a job going, and I would get to see this local hero, I wrote a letter applying for employment and received a courteous note asking me to call on the Saturday afternoon. I have to say that by then the village was beginning to have second thoughts about young Mr T, for suddenly his house had become filled with a very weird collection of arty people from London. How he had become embroiled with them was not known.

The house was a big old manor house, not very lovely, and with a lot of ugly carved wood in it. The ceilings were high, the fireplaces enormous and all the heat from the log fires went up the wide chimneys. I was interviewed in the hall, through which a cold draught blew lustily. As the only applicant I had no difficulty in securing the job at the princely wage of one pound a week; my hours were from 8 a.m. to 4 p.m. and I had to supply my own sandwiches.

My principal duty was the poultry, which, since the death of the old gardener/odd-jobman some six months previously, had been allowed to run wild. The job involved putting up proper pens, rearranging and creosoting the outhouses that the hens roosted in, and getting some new laying arrangements working. In addition to that, Mr T's little girl, now six, wanted a pony, and I was given the task of finding a suitable animal and teaching her to ride!

The hens were extremely annoyed at having their wayward lifestyle curtailed, so that once they were safely penned up, according to age and laying ability, all went on strike and the house was forced to buy in eggs from a local farmer until the sulky flock reluctantly resumed production. For the little girl's first pony I found a hairy brown Dartmoor gelding at a farmstead on the levels. It seemed quiet although only four, and my inexpert examination revealed no obvious blemishes. It cost twenty pounds, and they threw in saddle and bridle for an extra fiver. I perched the small girl on top to her immense glee, and each day when she came home from school I towed the two of them round the orchard. As I had to stay later than 4 p.m. to do this, I was paid an extra shilling.

During my weeks at the 'big house' I came in constant contact with Mr T's strange visitors: a mixture of painters, actors and poets, a well-known West End photographer who went everywhere with a sulphur-crested cockatoo perched on his shoulder; and various shadowy figures, some of whom wore long black raincoats that flapped at their heels, and were variously rumoured to be foreign or British spies—though what the latter would have been doing in a remote Somerset village was unclear. The leader of the band was a sultry, dyed redhead of indeterminate years who wore far too much make-up: an actress, I was told. That she had worked her wiles on the widower was very obvious, and I was constrained to remark to the postmistress that it was unlikely he would be visiting the graveyard at midnight for quite some time; a statement at which she pursed her mouth and turned quite pink, making some terse remark about 'Thik Lunnon hussey.' The 'Painted Lady', as she became known in our household had also taken over the upbringing of the little girl, and I often wonder how this sweet, innocent little soul as she was then, grew up.

The gang at Mr T's had taken over one of the big barns and transformed it, with the help of a local carpenter, into a small theatre in which they gave play readings, poetry evenings and, during the daytime, exhibitions of their pictures and photographs. No one in the village was invited except the doctor and the vicar, and the latter politely declined to enter the premises, and preached a rousing sermon on the dangers of original sin the Sunday after the invitation. The doctor was Irish, thirtyish, and devastatingly charming and had the females of all ages in the entire countryside madly in love with him. He enjoyed his theatre-going I was told. The theatre in the barn could be described as a transformed piece of old England. It was all hung with crimson velvet and had discreet lighting and looked exotic and possibly, if the word had been in common usage as it is today, erotic.

My time at Mr T's soon came to an end. After the hens were settled, and when a new, young would-be actress, who said she could ride, joined the household and offered to teach the little girl to ride properly, I had to go. The day I was leaving, the photographer invited me to his little flat for a cup of tea. The walls were hung with his work and as I was admiring some of the pictures the cockatoo gave a loud squawk, flew off its perch and alighting on my shoulder seized my ear lobe with its vicious beak. I grabbed it and, with blood pouring down my neck, whirled it round and threw it across the room; it landed on its feet, ruffled its feathers and launched itself at me. Fortunately I was near the door, and whipping it open

75

leapt through and slammed it behind me; it was satisfying to hear the thud as the bird hit the wood.

Although I left the job, I had not left all the occupants of the house behind. A pale-faced Austrian of 22 called Paul, with thin, yellow hair and watery, pale blue eyes behind round steel-rimmed spectacles, and an attitude of black despair, attached himself to my mother and me. He was always appearing on our doorstep with such an air of hopelessness that mother took him in and fed him. He had escaped ahead of the Nazis, who had captured all his family, and was waiting to see if he could get permission to go to America; in the meantime the slight, black-garbed figure tramped the lanes. Mother and I did our best to cheer him up a little, but although we got the occasional smile, he was a sad object, and when he finally received the all-clear to emigrate to the States we were not sorry to see him go. Imagine my surprise and horror to receive a long and impassioned letter declaring his love for me, written from shipboard. I was so embarrassed I threw it in the fire—and the last contact with the 'big house' was broken.

CHAPTER EIGHT

It was old Garge who provided the information that a farmer who lived on the hill about two miles away was wanting a temporary helper to do general work on the farm while his wife was having her first baby, and this gave me yet another macabre experience. Dolly being otherwise engaged, I walked the distance to the old red-brick farm and found my way to the back door. The Deans were a couple in their mid-thirties who had only married the previous year. She was a tall, gaunt woman with firmly anchored hair, a large-boned, hollow-cheeked face, a well-scrubbed complexion, and gimlet eyes; she also possessed very large feet. Her brown stuff frock was covered by a white, starched apron, of the bib variety favoured by farmer's wives of the period. Mr Dean was also tall, with a weather-beaten, red-cheeked face, a thin nose and small eyes. I did not like his look or his slack mouth.

Mrs Dean was heavy with child, but was still helping with the milking, and finding it pretty impossible to bend over her burden to reach the cows' teats. I was told that the baby was due in two weeks and, if it came on time, I should only be wanted for a month, as Mrs Dean intended to be back at work as soon as able: she and her husband did not believe in spending good money on outside help when they could do it all themselves. The pay was 30 shillings a week; I would be expected to arrive by 6:30 in the morning and I could leave at 5:30 in the evening. I said that I had no transport and asked if there was a bicycle I could borrow, but Mrs Dean had a better idea: she said that there were two ponies which did not get exercised, seeing the condition she was in, and that I could ride them, two turn and turn about, to my home and back, thus getting both ponies exercised and fit for when she resumed normal life again. I was delighted and, accompanied by Mr Dean, went out, caught, saddled and bridled one of the two Exmoor ponies, and rode home in high glee.

Riding up to the farm on the first morning, I thought how odd it was that the front part of the house seemed completely different from the back. There was a strand of barbed wire across the path that led round the house, and the front windows had a forlorn look, with no clean curtains like the windows at the back. There was a large wooden shed set in the front garden, which had long since gone back to the wild, and which contrasted strangely with the neat flowerbeds and prosperous vegetable garden on the far side of the premises. Being of an enquiring turn of mind I decided to investigate. The Deans were not a couple who engaged in much conversation, even between themselves, and certainly not the type to answer questions other than about work. I bided my time, and when the lady of the house finally took to her bed and the local midwife was called, I reckoned that Mr

Dean's attention might be otherwise engaged. That evening I rode as usual from the farm, but dismounted at the front gate and tied the pony to the one remaining gatepost.

Making my way towards the front of the house, the open door of the shed and the smell emanating therefrom caught my eye and nostrils, and I paused to look in. From floor to ceiling on all three walls were rabbit cages, one above the other. All the cages contained something: some had dung up to the roof; some had a dead rabbit, a half decomposed rabbit or a skeleton; and in some a few live rabbits crouched on mounds of dung. I was appalled. As I stood staring a voice said, 'You must be the little maid come to work on the farm,' and I turned to see an extraordinary apparition: Miss Dean, who I soon learned was the farmer's sister, was dressed in a style of the mid 1920s. She wore a brown and yellow frock with a round neck and wide hanging sleeves, and a dipped skirt to her knees. Over this she had a filthy grey cloth coat fastened low down on the left hip, once no doubt with a button, but now with a large safety pin; the tears where this anchor had been taken on and off were much in evidence. On her feet were much-worn boat-shaped shoes with the toes turned up, fastened by three bars and buttons across the instep. Pulled down on wispy grey hair was a cloche hat, anchored by a large hat pin which over the years had torn large holes in the felt. She was incredibly thin, but her wrinkled brown face was gentle and she had a nice smile.

The old lady volunteered that the rabbitry was in a bad

state, and said that her brother had sent for the RSPCA
man who had given her a week to clean things up, but she
did not know how she was going to manage. At 19 you
don't stop to think, and I at once offered my help, which
was readily accepted. I just hoped the offer would not
affect my regular job, as further conversation revealed that
brother and sister had hardly spoken for years; that Miss
Dean was only allowed to inhabit one half of the house as
a favour because she had nursed their mother through a
long, painful and terminal illness; and that as soon as her
brother could find an excuse she would be turned out.

Seeing that I was already at the farm and an hour or so
extra made no difference, as mother would feed the stock
anyway, I suggested that I make a start on the rabbitry. The
offer was gladly accepted, and finding an old spade I dug a
deep hole and started by burying all the dead. As the
manure was impacted so hard I did not manage to clear
more than four hutches before I deemed it time to go
home. However, Miss Dean insisted I go in for a cup
of tea. She led the way through the front door into
the hall, which was bare except for a drift of leaves
which had blown in, and large, black cobwebs that hung
down everywhere. It transpired that although she had two
bedrooms she lived entirely in the sitting room, sharing
this with nine assorted dogs, four cats and two cages of
doves. She told me that her brother forbade her ever to
take the dogs out, so they lived their life in the one room,
and when they made a mess or a puddle she simply spread
a sheet of newspaper over it, and trod it in; this meant
that on entering the room one stepped up quite eight

inches and appeared to be walking on solid papier-mâché! Although the cats performed in a box which she actually emptied, this did not improve the foetid air, while the muck and seed in the doves' cages was several inches deep.

A large table was covered in papers, magazines, letters, pieces of embroidery, empty cans and dirty cups and plates. There was a chaise longue backed against the wall opposite the window, and through slits in the Rexine covering lumps of black horsehair protruded; a few dirty blankets turned out to be the only bedding. A large carved mahogany sideboard, also covered in clutter, and two or three chairs completed the furnishings. The grate, in which a small wood fire was burning, housed a trivet on which a kettle steamed quietly. The tea was made in an old, cracked, brown pot and tasted surprisingly refreshing. I was sitting on a chair sipping the beverage and patting one of the dogs when I saw something move on the floor—yes, it was fleas actually hopping about! Leaving fairly hurriedly I promised to continue the work the next evening.

On arriving home I stood outside the back door and called to my mother to come out. She came, looking at my face curiously. 'Mother,' I grinned, 'we are back to the fleas again; get out the Keatings!' Although mother thought my story was exaggerated, she made me strip in the scullery and stand in the tin bath, fetched a kettle of warm water and handed me a scrubbing brush and a bar of carbolic soap, and when she came to examine my clothing she realised that fleas had indeed once again invaded our

81

lives. Every time I helped Miss Dean I had to go through this ritual when I came home, for as my mother said solemnly, with a twinkle in her eye, 'You would not want to give fleas to the Yorkies, would you!'

It took me about 10 evenings to get the rabbitry clean and this coincided with the return visit of the RSPCA man, who announced he was satisfied and departed not to be encountered again. By then the new mother, although 36, was up and about. I was not long in the job after that, as she was anxious to resume milking. So I turned the ponies back in their field with a farewell carrot each and was out of work again. Despite the fact that the Deans believed in getting their money's worth and had worked me hard, I had been quite happy in the job.

My friendship for Miss Dean, however, blossomed, she was such a lonely soul and would turn up several times a week riding her rusty old bicycle with the carbide lamp that had corroded and was encrusted with verdigris. When we saw her coming, mother would rush to sprinkle Keatings in the chair she would occupy, for it was possible to see the fleas walking on her clothing.

It was the postmistress who revealed the full story about Miss Dean. She had been personal secretary for many years to Mr T, the father of the estate agent for whom I had worked. She had been hopelessly in love with him and was convinced that he would ask her to be the second Mrs T; whether he was going to or not is an unsolved mystery, for he died of a sudden stroke only a year after his wife's demise, and his departure had a strange effect on his secretary. Life stopped for her, and from that moment on she dwelt, as it were, in a time capsule, wearing the same clothes, riding the same bicycle and totally ignoring the passage of time. We did not ask her about her life, but she volunteered various items at times, mentioning her old employer in glowing terms, but revealing nothing of any hidden passion.

Miss Dean had been a clever girl and had secured a place at the high school, so was well educated; it was a shame that she had been so ignored by the outside world and allowed to become a virtual recluse. Apart from her secretarial skills she was an expert needlewoman and it was also clear from her conversation that she was well versed in all farm chores and a good cook; yet she chose to live in abject poverty and appalling filth.

Only two months after we first became acquainted with Miss Dean, her brother told her to get out of the house. The doctor and the midwife had indicated that a baby should not live close to rooms in such an insanitary condition as Miss Dean's. She had to go. Give him his due, her brother found her a cottage that belonged to a farmer some seven miles away. It lay in the middle of the fields and did not even have a track to the door. The roof was unsafe and half the windows were without glass, but it was a refuge for her and her animals, and of course she asked me to help her move there.

The first task, she said, was to clear the bedrooms in her brother's house. I thought she meant of furniture, but when I opened the doors it was to find the floors two feet deep in old papers and magazines where she had thrown them over the years. These rooms had become cities of rodents, and whole dynasties of mice and the occasional rat had burrowed tunnels through the paper and made endless nests. As we stuffed the papers into sacks mice jumped out and ran in their dozens about the passage. It took nearly a week to clear the rooms and burn all the papers. Miss Dean's few pathetic possessions were loaded on to a borrowed farm cart, together with the cats in a box, and the cages of doves and rabbits, and sitting among them with her dogs she drove away and out of our lives.

It was at this time that I started contributing to the canine press with notes about the kennels in the area, and I became enmeshed in schemes to raise money for war charities. My first effort was an afternoon of pony rides. Although the mount was only Dolly, who was lent by old Garge 'to do 'er bit for the war,' some twenty children of various ages turned up and patronised the rides at a penny a go. They bought home-made rock buns from my mother for the same price and we raised nine shillings for the Red Cross. The next venture was rather more ambitious—a comic dog show. There were to be fourteen classes, starting with one for 'Farmers' dogs only' and another for 'Best looking gun dog', and continuing on through largest, prettiest, fattest, cleverest, etc. and ending with a rousing musical chairs with dogs. The whole thing took place in a large shed owned by the local garage. I managed to persuade Mrs Elma Stonex, the owner of a very famous Golden Retriever kennels, to be one of the judges, and a local lady volunteer to join her; both entered whole-heartedly into the spirit of the day. I scrounged around and wrote to several noted local dog breeders, and all the prizes had been donated and most of the expenses covered before the event. It was a true village affair, with the vicar opening the proceedings with a nice speech and a prayer, and the prizes presented by the Lady of the Manor wearing her best toque. Even the local bus company came up trumps, running a special service to and from Taunton just for the show. It was sixpence a time to get in and to enter a dog, and I led a miniature Shetland pony, bearing a money box attached to his saddle, around the assembled multitude at half-time. We raised the magnificent total of fifteen pounds, sixteen shillings and ninepence, which was sent to '*Our Dogs*' Fighter Fund. The event had quite a write-up in that paper as well as in the local press, which gave it much prominence, and it proved a flagship for many such shows later held up and down the county.

Mr Thomas kept a very small saddler's shop tucked away in a back street in the village. I used to go in just to watch him repairing saddles and bridles and to enjoy the good odour of fine leather and stale horse. He had for sale an old army saddle, the cantle and pommel of which were bound in brass. He only wanted two pounds for it, and I saved like mad and one day bought it and laboured home under its enormous weight. Mr Thomas was a kind man and had thrown in a pair of old leathers and rusty irons, as well as a much-worn webbing girth. The saddle sat badly on poor old Dolly's bony frame, so when I heard that a farmer had a horse that needed exercising, I set off, on foot of course, to find out more.

My destination was a big farm which lay down the hill and off the Taunton road, which meant a trek of some three miles. The farmer was an off-hand sort of chap, and all he told me about the horse was that his name was Sid and that he had been hunted. I did not bother to enquire further, but the next day walked the three miles again, this time carrying my heavy saddle. Sid was a chestnut with a wary eye. I hauled myself on him and at once realised that he was unlike any of the quads I had ridden before. He had an elastic step and was forward-going to the point of being uncontrollable. I rode him every day for a week, but never really felt much rapport with him.

Halfway through the second week we were out when Sid suddenly stopped dead still, up went his head, and his ears pricked up: in a nearby wood I heard the sound of the horn—hounds were about. Now one of my ambitions had always been to go hunting, but I really meant it to be in the correct manner. Sid had other ideas. We walked on quickly. The sound of hounds running came nearer and as we passed an open gate, Sid swerved inside, grabbed the bit and was away. I had just time to see the mounted field streaming across in front of us before we joined them. I was wearing Land Army breeches, rubber boots, a shirt and pullover, no hat, no coat, no gloves; and this with the whole immaculate field of the Taunton Vale around me. Well, there was nothing I could do except try and stay on as Sid was ploughing through the riders at an alarming rate, quite out of control. The end came as we swept through a muddy gateway: the saddle slipped sideways, and off I shot and away went Sid after the hounds.

Muddied from head to foot, I picked myself up to find an immaculate old gentleman with a stern, red face peering down from the back of his thoroughbred. 'Are you hurt?' he enquired. I shook my head, still out of breath. 'Where is your hat?' He looked round. I stammered out that I was not wearing a hat, and after giving me a long and incredulous stare, he rode off. Another gentleman of similar vintage caught the recalcitrant Sid, and waited while I adjusted the saddle and remounted. 'Better get him home,' he grunted turning away. I was only too happy to go home, but Sid was having far too much fun for that, and he pulled and tugged me into the road, where the field was clattering off, the hounds having lost the scent. Try as I might I could not stop the brute; weaving from one side to another he barged into other horses, and people swore at me as red-faced I tugged on the reins. At last rescue came in the shape of a crossroads. I hung grimly on to the left rein, pulling Sid in that direction by sheer brute force, and the field paused a few moments before going right. I managed to keep Sid straight and walking and eventually reached the farm. The horse had lost a shoe and I had lost my dignity. I collected my saddle and trudged home under the weight deciding to give Sid a miss in future.

If the gloomy Austrian's unexpected written declaration of love had caused a flurry in the household, that of Cecil Dark, which was more personal and nearer at hand, led to even greater consternation! Cecil was old Garge's nephew, a moon-faced youth of 20 with vacant blue eyes and an idiot smile. He worked on his father's farm and had an interest in horses, so old Garge brought him up to see me. 'Ceecil,' he said, for this was the way the family pronounced the boy's name, 'Ceecil do 'ave a young mare as 'e wants ridin', I said you was proper clever with 'osses.'

'Ceecil's' young mare proved to be half carthorse with a huge, ugly head and hairy heels. She had been broken—just—and he wanted me to ride her about to 'get 'er used to traffic like.' My saddle fitted her after a fashion, and she wore a cart bridle. Anything to ride was better than nothing, so I careered about on the mare for about two weeks, getting put through a thorn hedge when she took exception to a flapping tarpaulin on a passing lorry on the main road, and ploughing through someone's front garden when a car horn scared her. However, we came to no harm and she began to go quite well.

One evening after supper, Cecil arrived at the cottage door. He was clad in his best grey flannels, a tweed jacket and a new flat cap, in his hand he carried a long thin parcel. 'I come to give Miss this,' he said when my mother opened the door. She kindly invited him in and he thrust the parcel into my hands. It was a child's riding whip, very thin and incredibly frail, and from the pseudo-silver-mounted handle dangled a pale blue silk tassle. I had seen it in Mr Thomas's shop, priced at six shillings. Afraid that he would be offended if I refused, I made a grateful acceptance speech. Mother offered the visitor a cup of tea and he sat down on the edge of one of the chairs twirling his cap between his large, red, work worn hands. He stayed and he stayed, saying very little, and we almost had to throw him out at ten o'clock. It was the first of several such visits. However, the next day I rode his mare and carried the ridiculous whip and he was delighted.

Two days later he asked me to go to the pictures in Taunton on Saturday afternoon when there was a bus. I hastily thought up an excuse not to go. Then he called bearing a bunch of flowers, obviously filched from his mother's garden, and we realised that Cecil had come courting! My mother stepped in, and went to see his parents. I do not know what she said, but the visits ceased. I had a message by old Garge to say the mare did not want any more exercise, and from then on until we left the village, none of Jim Dark's family ever spoke to us again.

It was a bitter winter; mother was wracked with rheumatism but kept working at various tasks including her rabbitry now housed in the granary. Each day, as spring advanced, she trudged down to the levels with her sack, returning with it full of dandelions to add to the bran we managed to buy and the hay I had been given for doing odd jobs. We were desperately hard-up, the village shop had said no more credit, and I could not find regular work. There was only one thing for it—we had to leave the cottage. And so once again we sold up what we could, paid the bills and moved on.

CHAPTER NINE

The two Brown brothers wanted help on the farm. Their men had been called up and they had failed to find another male farm worker, and whether they liked it or not, and they obviously did not judging by their mutinous faces when I enquired about the job, they had been forced to turn to the Women's Land Army. It was through the bustling and busy woman who was in charge of the WLA in that area that I had heard about the Browns. This lady was the first I had met who had any notion of how to go about her task, and she whizzed around the county in a small and noisy car with great determination born of desperation with the intransigence of the farming menfolk.

The Browns' farm lay some three miles out of the small country town where we had gone to live, and once again I had no transport. I visited Curry's store, and for six guineas (a guinea was 21 shillings or £1.05) bought a brand new bicycle on hire-purchase—a few shillings down and two shillings a week! My wages of two pounds a week covered my hours from 6:30 a.m. to 6:30 p.m., six days a week, and I took my own sandwiches.

The Brown brothers were immense men, their great bodies straining at the heavy leather belts that held up their cord trousers, their waistcoats failing to meet across barrel-like chests, and their round blue eyes bulging out of the folds of fat red flesh on their faces. There was only a year between them and they could have been twins. They were loud and coarse, hard on the animals, and only kept in check by their fierce mother who ruled them and the farm with an iron hand—and no velvet glove. Mrs Brown had been widowed when her sons were quite small and since then had run the farm herself. She was a round, tightly corseted figure, always in a starched, white bibbed apron, with her grey hair wound up into a tight bun on top of her head. She had the same bulging blue eyes as her sons, and her mouth was crowded with the largest set of false teeth I had ever seen. These were so ill-fitting that they clicked and clacked as she spoke, and when she was eating they not infrequently got fastened into a piece of bread crust or fruit cake and refused to let go, whereon the old woman skilfully detached them from her mouth and pried off the offending ration.

The house was spotless; the meals gargantuan, and I used to sit at the breakfast table consuming my first packet of sandwiches and the cup of tea I had been grudgingly given, and watch as the great slices of home-produced fat bacon, the eggs and sausages, fried bread and mushrooms from the field out the back, went down with great draughts of tea and hunks of bread. At lunchtime I took to sitting out in the orchard for my meal as it was impossible to stay in while my employers chomped through platefuls of meat, gnawed bones and belched loudly after a handful of pickled onions.

The farm was quite large for the district, some 200 acres, but besides the brothers and myself, the only people left to work it were an old man, who did odd jobs part-time, and Rene, the girl who came twice daily to help with the milking. Rene was buxom and swarthy with more than a touch of the Romany in her jet-black hair, flashing eyes and merry laugh. I found her excellent company and when she asked me round for an evening after I had been a few weeks on the farm I was delighted. When I told my mother of the invitation she was adamant that there was no way I was going to spend the evening with someone she did not know! So I did not go, making such a feeble excuse that Rene shot me a knowing glance, smiled and said, 'Never mind.' Of course my mother had another motive for stopping my going: she knew far more than I did. Rene was quite a noted lady in the area, offering her not inconsiderable services to a wide circle of the male population. Maybe she had hoped to enlist me and enlarge her establishment!

The farmhouse and buildings were in a dip, and one had to walk up quite a steep track to the milking shed and dairy. This was yet another farm that had a dairy but no water, although we did strain the milk; it was then put in churns which we loaded on to the horse and putt for transport to the farmhouse. The back door of the house opened on to a long scullery, in which there was a deep stone trough about eight feet long and two foot six wide. The end of the room was furnished with a large iron pump, which was the only water supply for the house. The trough was half-filled with water and the churns stood in this with their lids cocked up, and this way the milk was cooled.

When the milk lorry had collected the churns in the morning I used to bring all the milking pails down and scrub them off in the same water in which the milk had been cooled. I used a large, slanted, heavy-bristled brush to scrub not only the interior clean of milk but the exterior clean of manure. When I had finished Mrs Brown would appear, seize the brush, and removing her false teeth give them a good scrub before briskly grabbing the pump handle and sending out a stream of icy water to rinse them. The first time she did this I stood amazed, thinking she was joking, but the dedicated look on her face and the practised way she wielded the bucket-brush told me otherwise and I found that this ritual was a daily occurrence. The dairy was the proud possessor of a galvanised bucket, into which one small kettle of hot water was poured with quite some ceremony when I took it down to the house before each milking. In this bucket we swilled the cloths to wipe the cows' udders. Of course, by the time we got the bucket up to the cowshed the water was nearly cold.

Both brothers, Rene and myself milked the 42 cow herd, mainly Shorthorns, and quite soon I found that after milking I would be left to clean the cowshed on my own. As no water was laid on, I firstly had to sweep all the dung and straw into piles and then load the barrow and push it out to the manure heap quite some distance away. By the time I had wheeled the twelfth or so barrow-load out, one of the brothers or the old man would have brought me two churns of water, and these had to be swished in bucketfuls over the floor, which I then swept until it presented a semblance of cleanliness.

Summer and the weather was hot. The Brown brothers in their local pub, where they drank heavily each evening, had boasted how they had a 'bit of a maid' working for them, and how they were going to break her heart—that would teach the women to think they could do men's work. I suppose all the years that their mother had run the farm and worked alongside the men had gone for naught. The pronouncement, of course, reached my ears. I determined that no matter how hard they worked me they would not win—but it was a close-run thing.

The farm boasted three bulls, each one more stroppy than the next. They lived in separate pens in which they roamed loose, and quite early on I was given the job of feeding them and seeing to their water. The most fearsome was a big, red bull who must have weighed a ton and a half. He had a huge head with forward-jutting horns and a bellow loud enough to wake the dead. He would wait at the end of the barn in which he was shut until I was inside with hay and feed, and then roar and start towards me, head lowered. Fortunately, I always managed to nip out in time.

The calves, of which there were around 24, jostled for food and attention in another barn; none, not even the youngest, were kept separately. It was a question of survival of the fittest. I had to go in with three buckets of milk on either arm and fight my way amongst them until the right heads were in the right buckets. My hands and arms were covered in cuts and bruises by the end of a week and my feet had been well trodden on.

As I never complained I suppose the brothers thought they were losing the battle and determined to find me other more difficult tasks. I was relieved of bulls and calves, and armed with a staff hook they sent me off to trim hedges round the orchards and 'get they nettles down.' A staff hook is a fearsome weapon that is used for trimming tree branches—rather like a billhook but attached to a long, thick handle. It is heavy and requires a great deal of expertise for effective and safe use. The old odd-jobman materialised by my side as I trudged off to the orchard, and in a husky whisper said he would come and show me 'how thik thing was best managed,' and under his expert help I soon got the hang of the 'slasher' as he called it. It was wicked weather for trimming round the orchards, and the sweat rolled off me in gallons. A week of this work, plus the milking and fetching the cows in every afternoon, nearly a mile and a half back and forth across the fields, and I was beginning to feel the strain. If I had been left on this work longer, the Browns must have won, but they were impatient for success and sought to break me by changing me to what they considered a more challenging job.

It was time for sheep dipping, and so I was put to this, and given a long pole to push the wretched animals' heads under the thick, grey mixture as they swam through the dip. As I was positioned near the end, I got a full blast of the wet sheep as they shook wildly on emerging, which pleased my tormentors greatly, and I smelt terrible when I got home. The next job the brothers came up with was horse hoeing. The horse hoe is rather like a single-furrow plough only lighter. The hoe, which is steadied by a man walking behind, is drawn by one horse in trace chains which is led down the furrows. It was my job to lead the horse, up and down, up and down in the broiling sun between the rows of roots. I could only comfort myself that at least I was with a horse, and that singling beet by hand with a hoe in a ten acre field was a far more soul-destroying job.

It was at this point that AJ came along. AJ was a dairy farmer with some fifty acres of rented grazing land and a clutter of farm buildings two miles nearer the town than the Browns' establishment. He was a producer-retailer and delivered milk daily from a pony and float. AJ was one of a large farming family who went back generations in the folklore of the area. He had a younger brother with a similar operation who worked a similar area of land on the opposite side of town, and his milk round and that of AJ's divided the town into two halves and two factions. The brothers, so alike to look at and in manner, were barely on speaking terms—some family feud it appeared, but when asked, all the locals became remarkably tight-lipped. Both men were tall and spare, with rugged faces and small black eyes. They dressed alike, in tan cavalry twill breeches, black gaiters and hobnailed boots, tan-coloured Harris tweed jackets and caps of the same material. When a float swept past you in the town, only the difference in the initials on the side told you whether it was AJ or AH driving.

AJ delivered milk to the flat and shop that my mother, after several rented rooms, had managed to get unfurnished for a modest pound a week. Mother had quickly decided that she could not have an empty shop, so set about making it into a place where made-to-order clothes for children and ladies' underwear could be sold. She would disappear up to London by train to visit wholesalers and return with velvets and satins, needles and lace and all manner of embroidery silks—heaven only knows how she got them in wartime—and sit stitching away for hours. Her best-seller was a blue velvet suit for little boys, and at one time the toddlers in the town became almost clones as they paraded with their parents through the town on Sunday in one of mother's specials.

My spaniels had proliferated, the Yorkies were still with us, and we had been joined by a large ginger cat who turned up one day and refused to leave, so we christened him Ernest as he wanted to stay so earnestly. Our dwelling was in the main street; very old and in bad repair. Behind the shop there was a sitting room, a cubby hole for the cooking stove, and a dank, dark scullery leading to a small yard enclosed by a high wall. Upstairs we had two large rooms, a small one and a WC. There was no bathroom so the tin tub was in use again, only this time we did have an old and rusty gas cooker on which to boil up the buckets of water.

AJ used to stop each day and have a cup of tea and chat to mother when he delivered our milk, as the shop was halfway through his round. He had heard that I was working at the Browns, and one evening came and banged on the shop door. When I answered he came directly to the point as was his way: 'How do you like working for they Browns?' I had to admit that I was not all that amused by it, whereon he offered me a job on his farm. The pay was two pounds six shillings a week, four shillings would be deducted for insurance, etc., and two free pints of milk a day. I had to work six days a week and some Sunday mornings with no extra pay. He understood I liked horses and could ride: well, he had a hunter and all the work was done by horse and cart, and he bought and sold a few and would appreciate someone who was interested.

That Saturday I had great pleasure in telling the Browns I would not be coming back . . . ever. I treasure the look on their faces to this day.

AJ lived with his wife and daughter in a cosy cottage in a village on the other side of town. The cottage stood on a bit of land with the inevitable orchard of cider apples; some pigsties in which AJ fattened porkers; several hen houses for the collection of barnyard fowls who laid large brown eggs mostly in the clumps of nettles that sprouted unheeded from every corner; and a shed for the hound puppies which he 'walked' each year for one or other of the hunts. There was also a stable for the float in which AJ drove home each night. Mrs AJ was a dear. A thin, wiry woman in the regulation white apron, she worked as hard as anyone; AJ was addicted to the local cider and his friends were legion, so much of the work with the pigs and fowls fell to her. She also tended a good vegetable garden, grew pretty flowers and kept her kitchen spotless and the table groaning with good, home-cooked food. Their daughter was a pale-faced, dark-haired girl for whom AJ had great plans. She was not brought up to work on the farm, but had stayed on at high school where she had done well, and had just started her first job as a typist in the office of a local solicitor. She seldom came up to the farm where I worked unless her cousin Ray, on whom she had a bit of a crush, was there.

The job I had taken on had been created by the departure of AJ's niece who had worked for him for some time, and I pondered long and hard as to why AH's daughter should work for her uncle, seeing that the two brothers were at loggerheads. I tried unsuccessfully to pump AJ's unmarried sisters who still lived in the old family farmhouse at the edge of the town, but I did not get very far, so it was left to my fertile imagination to find a solution. It did trickle out that the takings from the milk round had not added up correctly on a few occasions, and I wondered if Nancy had been put there to effect industrial sabotage on AJ's enterprise, but that did not explain how AJ had come to take her on in the first place. Whatever the situation had been, Nancy went and I took over.

There were 18 to 20 cows in milk at any one time. We milked them in a long wooden shed with a felted roof, and no electricity. In winter we set lighted candles along the beams and sat on our stools in the flickering flame, morning and evening, singing and laughing and telling tall stories.

When there was deep frost or snow the cows lived in

all the time; this made an enormous amount of extra work cleaning up behind them, for we had no loose yard and they spent sometimes three months chained in their stalls with just a leg-stretching exercise in the small yard each day. What a laugh when they were at last turned free in the fields again: great ungainly creatures galloping and frisking with bags swinging wildly to slap their sides, bucking and kicking they went round the field until settling to pull at the grass. The milk yield always plummeted at first after this exercise, and then climbed to the highest yields of the year as the good spring grass began to take effect.

In the summer the cows were hot, and damp with sweat; they were also full of good, green grass and spread it lavishly over our faces and clothes as with their tails they swiped the endless clouds of flies that settled on their backs. In bad weather they came in, water running off their bodies and mud up to the hocks. Bags were covered in mud and required a great deal of washing off, and our right shoulders and arms that came in contact with the beasts as we milked were soon sodden with rain and mud, to say nothing of our milking caps as we pressed our heads against the streaming sides.

The dairy, made of ageing asbestos, had gone green inside and out for half its height, and outside it stood a large copper, which had to be primed with wood and paper and set alight every morning to boil water for the bottle-washing which I did on my return from the milk round. Once again we had the part-time services of an elderly man, Sam, who was so emaciated that his ancient garments appeared to walk of their own accord. His craggy old face was surmounted by an old felt hat, and he wore ragged mittens on hands knotted dreadfully by arthritis. He came and went at will, so it was never possible to rely on him. He was supposed to both muck out the stalls and light the copper, but he usually did one or the other. To come back with a load of empty bottles and find no hot water was annoying, as if I had to light up and wait for the water to heat, it set me back at least an hour.

The cowshed was at right angles to the dairy and copper, and against its wooden wall stood a high-legged, double-galvanised tank in which the bottles were washed. One side took the hot water which I bucketed from the copper; the other was filled by a hosepipe from the tap. The powder used in the water for cleaning the bottles could skin hands less hardy than mine, and the plunging of glass bottles from hot to cold water, especially on frosty days, was hazardous as many would split and it was easy to cut oneself badly. The empty crates stood around in the mud of the yard, the clean bottles being put back in them upside down to drain, and were when full stacked on the small, pitted concrete area in front of the dairy. It was, on reflection, not the most hygienic way to go about things, but none of our customers ailed from drinking our milk.

AJ and I did the milking twice a day—10 or 11 cows each. They were a motley crew and comprised specimens of various breeds. There was Granny, the Jersey, who was all of 18 years of age, and who slipped twins each year, but gave beautiful, rich milk. She was one of the most difficult from which to abstract milk—hard teats they said—which meant the milking ducts were restricted and one had to pump and squeeze for quite a time until her capacious bag was empty—it played hell with the wrists. Carnation was a Guernsey who was so easy to milk that any spare hands who turned up to help always bagged her first. Two bottles of milk from either Granny or Carnation were always saved each morning and placed in known positions in a certain crate in both milk floats, so that if we were stopped on either round by the milk inspector, we could give him this bottle in the sure and certain knowledge that it would not fail any of the tests!

As well as Granny and Carnation, there were Rusty and Tulip, both Shorthorns. Rusty got bloat and AJ stuck his knife in her just in front of her hip bone, and the air that shot out in a jet stream smelt like nothing on earth. Despite drenches and the doubtful ministrations of the old vet, Rusty went to the slaughter house. Tulip was also unfortunate as she contracted Johnes, a wasting disease, and got thinner and thinner despite all the various con-coctions we poured down her unresisting throat. 'No good for aught but glue,' said AJ at last, and Tulip was collected next day.

Kicker, the third Shorthorn, was made of sterner stuff than the others. A massive cow, she gave a tremendous yield; otherwise she would never have been tolerated. Unless AJ was absent through illness, which was seldom, or off to a meet of the staghounds on his big horse Gilbert, which in the season was often, AJ always milked Kicker himself. I dreaded his absence, for nothing anyone else could do to Kicker could stop that wicked hind leg with the power of several elephants from sending milker, bucket and stool sailing down the cowshed. We tried putting the span on her legs, tying the milking-side hind leg to the back partition, putting on the bulldogs (a pair of iron tongs on the nose), and stringing her head up to the overhead beam, and placing a rope over her back (an old-fashioned remedy for fidgety cows)—all of which had little or no effect. There was also a small black Dexter whose large bag was so close to the floor that it gave anyone who milked her backache; Polly the red poll who chased people round the field when she had a calf; Patch the Friesian, a cow of little charm; and many more.

After the demise or sale of a cow, AJ used to take me down to the local market and leave me to choose a replacement. '*You* got to milk 'em,' he would grin, '*you* choose 'em, and mind you choose right.' And off he would go to the Market Inn for cider with his friends. Solemnly I would go up and down the line of cows for sale, chatting to the vendors and hearing all the marvellous tales about their animals, and wondering, if they were such paragons, why they were for sale.

Observing the shape of the udder, and seeing that the teats were evenly placed, I would squat down beside a likely purchase and try the teats to find out if they were easy or hard to milk and all the same size; one teat smaller than the rest could be 'blind' from injury or mastitis. I learned to look for a glossy coat and good skin, clear eyes, and good feet. A cow needs to be well built and stand well, and her top line has to be as level as possible and the

103

bag properly attached if she is to be a good milker. Cows were expected to give many years' service in those days, so durability was much desired.

When I had made my selection I used to send a message to AJ. Girls in pubs were not the thing then, except girls of a 'certain kind' as my mother would have said, and the rowdy crowd of farming men would have been vastly embarrassed if I had put foot in the pubic bar. AJ would come out to inspect my choice and either approve or disapprove. He knew all the farmers for miles around, and their stock, and sometimes I would choose a cow from a doubtful vendor, and then hurriedly have to find something else. Fresh-calved cows fetched anything from £20 to £35 then, and AJ reckoned £29 was our limit. When he had purchased the desired animal in the auction, he arranged for the delivery of the new possession and went back in the pub while I went back to the farm to arrange for the arrival of the newcomer and settle her in.

Cattle have a very cruel streak. They are herd animals and object strongly to any newcomer trying to join them. Our new arrival would suffer the sharp horns of her new companions as they jostled her about the field and hooked her unmercifully when she inadvertently blundered into the wrong stall. This sort of behaviour lasted about two weeks and then they ostracised her, and she would graze unhappily alone, while every now and then one of the herd would look in the direction of the hated newcomer, raise her head and bellow an insult. It was fair to say that every new cow took at least a month, sometimes more, before she became an accepted member of the herd.

We had little trouble with calving: an expectant mother would retire to a secluded corner of the field accompanied by an 'auntie' or 'midwife cow', and deliver her offspring without human interference. When the calf was born the 'auntie' would bellow the news of the arrival to the rest of the herd, and they would all troop over and stand round blowing and dribbling and nudging each other, eyes bulging as they surveyed the little wet creature being licked by two cows and struggling to get on its legs and round to the waiting milk bar. Once or twice we had a cow in trouble and she would be brought into the spare shed, but I fear the accouchement was not as scientific as it is today, as a rope would be attached to whichever leg of the calf was available, and all hands tugged and pulled as the cow heaved. Sometimes the vet came, but his methods were little different, although he did turn the calf's head or legs when they were lying in the wrong direction so that it was better presented and likely to slide out easier, giving the calf a better chance of survival, and the cow less likelihood of being badly torn. Retained afterbirth trailing behind a cow had a brick tied to it by a length of binder twine; it was reckoned that the added weight would cause the membrane to dislodge itself—strangely this method often worked. We once had an outbreak of contagious abortion, which affected four cows only. The aborted foetus was buried with lime, and the place where the abortion took place in the field was covered in straw and petrol and set alight to cleanse it of infection.

AJ took the old residential side of our area for delivery of the milk, whereas I had the largest area. My customers consisted of some of the poorest in the town, some of the shopkeepers and part of a select residential district. It was a great way to learn about human nature. The poorest people came out with their few coppers regularly each Saturday, the shopkeepers paid each month and the residentials owed. Some of the older customers would not have their milk in bottles, so I had to carry a small churn on board and one of those lovely oval, brass-bound pails with a lid and a rail inside on which hung pint and half-pint measures. The women would bring their jugs to the door and have their milk measured out in the time-honoured fashion, and woe betide the operator who did not give the expected 'drop extra'.

The wide street with sloping sides that led to the town had once been the marketplace. On the left side was a continuous terrace of red-brick cottages, the little alley-ways between them leading to yards in which were situated communal wash houses and privies. In this row lived a number of very old and intensely poor people, and the squalor of their dwellings and the stench live with me yet. They were pathetic old souls who dearly loved a chat, and I often took precious time to go in for 'a cup 'o tea dearie,' and enjoyed their company for, although their lives were hard and many of them were far from well, they were all extraordinarily cheerful and had wonderful stories to tell. AJ, in spite of his rough and bluff exterior, had a heart of gold, and when he knew one of the old people was ill would tell me to leave extra milk and not charge—usually the old dears only had one of those tiny quarter pints twice a week.

On the other side of the street the houses were larger, taller, better kept and had their own yards and facilities. They were occupied by people who worked in the town, who had a connection with agriculture or who had retired. Old Widow Clark was one of these. Her husband had been a farmer of some consequence, and when he had died leaving her comparatively well off but with no children, she had sold up and bought a house with a large garden on the outskirts of town. Old habits die hard, and Widow Clark, who had always had a great name for her cream and butter, had a small dairy built in the garden, and by buying in milk continued to produce her much-sought-after products from her new abode. By the time I knew her she was a very old lady indeed, with a long black dress, spotless white apron and a crochet snood to hold her thinning locks in place.

Twice a week I delivered several gallons of milk from Granny and Carnation, from which Widow Clark made cream and butter. She was a very cheerful old soul with rosy cheeks and always had a steaming-hot cup of cocoa ready for me when I called. One summer day when I was sitting in her cosy kitchen sipping my drink and looking out at the flowers in the back garden through the open door, I noticed that the dairy door was open, and that her black cat was up on the slate slab with the pans of milk in which the cream set. 'Mrs Clark,' I said quietly, 'your cat is in the dairy.' I could see Puss perched on the side of a pan. 'Oh, don't take n' notice, m'dear, he do often go in for a little drink.' 'But Mrs Clark,' I protested, 'that is not the end that is over the pan!' She gave a little laugh. 'Oh, he do often do that m'dear, not to mind, I can soon spoon it out!'

Cocoa was a hazard all along my route; people were very kind and especially in bitter winter months thought that a hot drink would warm me up. So many had the same idea, and not wishing to hurt feelings I used to drink up all the offerings, that by the time I got back to the farm I was awash with the stuff. The first cup came early when I called on AJ's sisters whose house was the first on the round. This had been a farmhouse but the land had been sold up, and the two sisters, tall and gaunt like their brothers, with severe faces and hair pinned back into neat buns, had just retained the orchard and a large productive garden where they also kept a pen of fowls.

The house was spotlessly clean and I had to remove my boots before going into the kitchen. No dogs or cats were allowed indoors, but there was an old balding parrot in a cage in the parlour. The bird had belonged to their mother, and for her sake it was kept and tolerated, but was heartily disliked by the pair, at whom it swore in awful tones. AJ used to stump into the kitchen, boots, mud and all, with his sisters clucking disapproval and laying sheets of newspaper for him to tread on. He infuriated them by tramping into the parlour and annoying the parrot, who would shriek and swear and shake its elderly plumage until some of its remaining feathers flew out of the cage on to the highly polished linoleum or the handmade rag rugs.

The sisters apparently provided a bridge between the feuding brothers, for both AJ's daughter and AH's offspring called there, and should communication between the brothers be desired, it was conducted via messages left with their sisters.

Mr Bowden, the dustman, lived opposite the sisters. He was a giant of a man with a kind heart, and was always about helping the old people in the terrace but in such a discreet way that only those who called on them regularly, such as myself, were aware of the situation. Mr Bowden worked long, hard hours on the dustcart, and in the evenings took on spare jobs. He lent a large hand at haymaking time, and his jovial presence and hearty laugh were most welcome.

Mr Bowden had a son of about eight: a streetwise urchin with spiky blonde hair, and a wide, cheeky grin. Known as Young Bowden, he was a terror in school and played the schoolmaster up so much that the cane was frequently in use—which dismayed him not at all. He was a cheerful sinner, scrumping apples, tying the knockers on people's doors together, and hanging on to the backs of lorries as they went down the street, scuffing his heavily nailed boots on the road as he went. There was, however, no actual harm in the lad; he was just a boy full of devilry and high spirits and as long as he was aware that discipline lurked in the background he was manageable. Quite an entrepreneur in his way, he earned many a copper doing all kinds of odd jobs and thinking up useful schemes to top up his income. On most Saturday mornings he came on the milk round with me, and received a shilling from

AJ. He was smart and quick and enabled me to get through on time. Saturday was pay-day for the milk bills and if I did not have Young Bowden with me I got back to the farm much later than on other days. I often wonder what happened to the boy. I think he either ended up a millionaire or in jail—perhaps both!

CHAPTER TEN

Gilbert was the most important thing on the farm, and possibly in AJ's life, his wife and daughter coming a poor second and third. Gilbert was a huge horse of some 17.2 hands. The story was that his mother was a cart mare who escaped and got in with an imported American trotting stallion living in a nearby field. Gilbert was a bright bay, with a huge, cart-type head and large, intelligent eyes. Although his frame was immense there was quality about him, and his well-boned legs were not coarse, but he did have enormous feet. He was a kindly soul and we became great friends, and when he was out in the field by the track would come galloping across as soon as I rang my bicycle bell when I turned up at the farm in the early mornings.

I was quickly given the job of strapping Gilbert, although I had to stand on a milk crate to reach his back and the top of his head. He was called after a huntsman with whom AJ was great friends, and when the conversation turned to the pack and the horses it was difficult to know to which Gilbert AJ was referring. Stag-hunting starts in August so Gilbert had to be fit and ready, and one year AJ had the bright idea of exercising his horse between the shafts of the milk float.

Gilbert had never been broken to harness—to say that delivering milk behind him was hair-raising is to put it mildly. AJ soon found that Gilbert was not going to stand still outside houses, so I held a carrying crate full with six bottles and hung on the back step, dropping off as the float reached a customer's house, and leaping aboard again as it passed at speed for the second time. After ten days of this AJ decided to give it best: he was missing good drinking time. So Gilbert returned to being exercised in the more orthodox way, which meant I went back each evening and rode him out.

One evening in the autumn when I was riding Gilbert down a lane, I heard a fluttering in the hedge. Dismounting I tied the horse to a gate, and on investigation found an injured cock pheasant in the tangle of brambles. Food was valuable in wartime, and pheasants found injured by gunshot belonged strictly to the owner of the land on which they were shot. I looked round. There was no one in sight; so I quickly despatched the bird and buttoned the carcass inside my jacket, remounted and rode back to the farm, hugging myself with the thought of a couple of good dinners to come and no one any the wiser. But there were eyes everywhere in the country in those days, and a week later an old farm worker, meeting me as I drove the cows across to the water meadows, said with a twinkle, 'Enjoy thik pheasant then?' I had, of course, not thought to remove the long tail feathers of the bird, and they had stuck out under my coat; the old man, busy in his garden as I rode past, had spotted them with his sharp countryman's eyes.

Gilbert could only be exercised on his own: he had a long stride at walk, but his trot was obviously inherited from his sire: while everything else was galloping, Gilbert could keep up with them at his long, swinging trot. It was impossible to go on a hack with a mounted companion for I would have been half a mile in front in less than no time, so I always went alone on Gilbert.

All paragons in the animal kingdom have to show some faults like ordinary creatures, otherwise they would be unbearable, and Gilbert was no exception: he would not allow himself to be mounted from the ground by the rider placing a foot in the stirrup—you had to climb aboard from a block or gate. As only AJ and myself ever rode him that was all right—until Metford came up for a ride. Metford, who kept a local pub, was one of AJ's closest friends, liked a ride and often took out one of the numerous horses or ponies that passed through AJ's hands in the course of the year, for a hack or day's hunting. He suddenly announced that he wanted to ride Gilbert, and AJ, much to my surprise, agreed. Metford came up resplendent in his batwing breeches, brown gaiters and boots, check jacket and bowler hat.

Gilbert was saddled and ready. 'Met,' called AJ from under a cow in the shed, 'don't try and mount him from the ground, climb up on the gate or some crates.' Metford smiled. I led Gilbert out and handed him over, horrified to see the man pull down the leather and prepare to place his foot in the stirrup. 'Don't do that,' I cried. 'Get on from the gate.' Metford knew better and placing his foot in the iron grabbed the horse's mane and hauled himself up. It all happened so quickly that it was not until the splintering sound of wood reached our ears that we saw the result of Metford's disobedience. As he had hauled himself aboard, Gilbert had doubled up his giant frame and gone up like a coiled spring: Metford had shot across the saddle and crashed headfirst through the rotten boards at the base of the cowshed to end up in the dung channel with a broken collarbone and a smashed wrist and rip down his cheek—he was lucky not to be far more badly injured. It was the end of Metford's equestrian activities for quite some time, but it provided much mirth and merriment in the telling in the public bar, so I was told, and the poor man was the butt of innumerable jokes. Once mended, Metford resumed riding and hunting, but he never again requested to go out on Gilbert.

Shaddock, Bob and Violet were the three driving ponies. Shaddock was known as my mare, and was a sour old thing with long yellow teeth, and feet which had been badly affected by laminitis at some stage in her life. She stood on her heels and was plainly uncomfortable: when left outside the houses on the round she rocked back and forth making the crates slide from the front to the back of the float so she could not be left long or the rear crate would crash to the ground. She hated people: most in the little town knew her, and when she was parked gave her a wide berth; the less wary found their sleeve caught in a vice-like grip while she flattened her ears and rolled her eyes in fury. Shaddock and I became great friends. I was possibly the only person she never bit; even AJ had felt the power of those yellow fangs on occasion.

Once a week the bins were put out to be emptied by Mr Bowden and his accomplices; this was Shaddock's chance, and when I called at a house she would set off, overturning bins and searching the contents for dainty morsels to eat. Once when delayed at a house on dustbin day, possibly for cocoa, I came out to find that Shaddock had reached the end of the street, and that every single bin was on its side, the contents all over the place; she must have zigzagged from one side to the other leaving no bin unmolested. Various ladies came out and shouted at me, and one or two even shook their fists at the mare. On another occasion as we turned up the rise to the farm track the belly band and breeching broke and the float tipped up, shooting not only the driver but the crates of empties on to the ground; Shaddock, completely oblivious, trotted on to the farm leaving a cursing driver and a trail of broken glass. Another time, backed up to the dairy so that I could load the crates, she was gently rocking, as was her way, and suddenly gave an extra heave and put the float through the side wall of the dairy.

In icy weather the frost nails with which all the horses and ponies were shod were of no use to Shaddock, owing to the shape of her foot, so I had to bind her hooves up in sacking and lead her on the round, very often having to support her whole weight if she lost her footing. Shaddock, at 15 hands the biggest of the three working ponies, was also expected to pull the light wagon, the swathe turner or the horse rake at haymaking time. She loathed the last two jobs, possibly thinking them beneath her dignity, and once, when we were amiably, as I thought, turning the sweet-smelling swathes of newly cut grass, she took off for no obvious reason, and horse, driver and swathe turner ended up half jammed in the gateway and half in the ditch. She was so obstreperous when requested to pull the chain-harrow that we often had to leave the job to the 14.2 hands cob, Bob.

Bob was another bay and he had been a hunter. His manners were good, but he suffered badly from wind, and was frequently known to expel this when being driven through an area thick with pedestrians, sticking his short docked tail straight up and emitting loud explosions for several minutes, causing roars of laughter from small children, rude remarks from men, and bringing a blush to many a female cheek. When Shaddock was required for farm work I was given Bob to drive, and found his behaviour always true to form! I also used him in what was termed the 'pig cart', a box-like contrivance on two pneumatic tyres, to get back home at lunch time. Bob and the pig cart were tied to a lamppost in a side road, while I had a hurried meal, and then, three times a week, we set off for the town brewery where we collected hot grains for feeding to the cows. A large metal shute extended from the brewery buildings and down this the grains cascaded in a smoking, odorous mass. If I arrived before the signal was given to open the door to the shute, it was possible to back the cart under the shute and get it filled easily; if I were late, I had to fill the cart by hand using a wide metal shovel, which was heavy and time-consuming work. In winter it was grand to drive back with rubber-booted feet warming nicely in the hot grains; but in summer it was agony! Once back at the farm the grains were tipped into two large iron baths that AJ had acquired from somewhere, and morning and evening the cows received a ration to go with their other short feed of cake and meal.

Bob and the pig cart also did the job for which the contraption was originally made: namely, conveying the porkers to market. It could hold two large pigs comfortably, three at a pinch. The driver, forced to stand up front and tied in tightly by the pig netting put over the top to stop the occupants jumping out, risked getting legs crushed or bitten—pigs have very sharp teeth which they will not hesitate to use if put in a situation not to their liking. Once, halfway to market, the binder twine holding the pig netting to the slatted side of the cart broke, and the sole occupant, apart from myself, made a dive for freedom. I concluded the trip hanging grimly on to one of the creature's ears while steering Bob with the other hand.

Bob went on AJ's round each morning. He was a horse of strange tastes. He once ate AJ's straw hat, leaving only the hatband to show it had ever existed, and he liked nothing better than ripping cloth. Woe betide the unwary who left an unguarded jacket in the yard; if Bob was there, the jacket would, in AJ's own words, 'be torn to libbets.' One day AJ, stopping for his usual chat and a drink at the local tailors, left Bob outside parked behind one of those old Austin 7 cars with a canvas roof. When he eventually returned to duty, it was to find Bob asleep on his feet, lashes on his hairy cheeks and a beatific smile on his whiskery lips. The roof of the car was indeed 'in libbets'. 'What did the owner say?' I asked curiously when AJ told the story on reaching the farm. 'Didn't stop to arsk!' was the reply, as with a grin he unharnessed the unrepentant cob.

Violet was an Exmoor mare of great age and a favourite with Mrs AJ, who kept saying that she should be retired, but Violet was far too valuable for she was in effect AJ's chauffer. It was Violet, harnessed to the pig cart, who took AJ out on his evening peregrinations round the local pubs. She knew them all, and, should I drive her on some errand, she slowed up of her own accord at every watering hole patronised by her owner, sometimes stopping dead and refusing to move. This signalled that the establishment was kept by a publican with a family addicted to horses, and Violet well knew that if she stopped, a crust of bread or carrot would be forthcoming for her refreshment.

Most nights AJ finished up the worse for wear. His mates would bundle him into the pig cart, where he would lie singing bawdy songs or sleeping deeply, sometimes on his back with his legs in the air. Having tied the reins to the rail of the cart, someone would give Violet a slap on the rump and command her to get 'the old boy home', a command instantly obeyed, and the local constabulary were well used to seeing the little mare trotting slowly back home with her owner lying incapable in the cart. The old mare could do all the jobs on the farm and was useful for transporting light loads, for drawing the milk float if one of her companions was needed elsewhere, for riding down to the water meadows to fetch in the cows, and for chain-harrowing, a task she seemed to enjoy. When she eventually got too old for farm work, AJ gave her to the local convent where she drew the small roller over the smooth, green lawns and was much petted and spoiled by the nuns.

Many other horses and ponies passed through AJ's hands while I was there including Jack, Hasty and Damsel: through each I learned new horse-riding skills. Jack was a big, old heavyweight hunter whom I found difficult to master because of my lack of experience. Hasty, a horse of good schooling and impeccable manners, was a joy to ride. She was the first properly trained horse I had come across and through her I became a much better rider.

Damsel was a lean, fast racing pony whom I had always wanted to take hunting. When I asked AJ about it he gave a sly smile and said that I could if I was 'so minded'. It was a long-cherished ambition of mine to go hunting and I had already kitted myself out. The local tailor had supplied me with a decent pair of cavalry twill breeches for all the clothing coupons I could spare and extra milk on the side (it was then rationed). The local menswear shop had come up with a strange-shaped bowler to fit my rather large head. I acquired a second-hand tweed 'rat catcher' jacket and my mother paid for an elegant pair of black-top boots, again second-hand, which were a size too small, took hours to get into, looked marvellous and were unendurable to wear until my feet had gone quite numb with shock.

I sewed a silk cord to the brim of the bowler and attached the other end to my buttonhole. I had never ridden in a hat and guessed it would blow off—and I was right: it spent most of the time bobbing on its cord against my back while I struggled with reins and handkerchief, as my nose always streamed when I was on a galloping horse.

My day's hunting was wild and uncontrolled, Damsel was so narrow that it felt as if I only had a slice of paper between my knees, especially since I was used to cobs and the bigger horses. I must have looked a sight rocking and rolling in the saddle as I strove to pull her up out of her headlong gallop, for Damsel thought every change of pace signified a race and she was determined to be first. (Damsel was really the only horse I ever rode who could keep up with Gilbert.) Her first great leap forward was when she saw a dead snake lying across the path on our way to finding the action, and it took me quite some yards to pull the terrified mare back to a trot.

When we really got going, AJ, who rode through and over anything on Gilbert, the two being quite fearless, plunged headlong down one of the coombes for which west country hill ranges are famous. He went on through a bog at the bottom and up the other side, to charge through a plantation of young trees, the stems whipping his and the following riders' legs and faces with a fearful stinging action. Damsel was on Gilbert's heels all the way. I was fortunate not to take a tumble, and I never again requested the racing pony as a mount for hunting!

Another memorable hunt was that in which I rode Dobbin. He was a small, fat cob (named after those old Victorian rocking horses because of his grey colouring)

120

with a stubborn streak. It was this obstinacy which made AJ anxious to sell Dobbin and he suggested that I ride the cob and accompany him when he and Gilbert went hunting, as the horse might behave well enough to attract a likely buyer. We were never able to get to a meet as the milking (although done over an hour earlier on such occasions) and the milk delivery (no empties picked up on hunting days) both had to be finished before we rode off. It was a ludicrous partnership and we must have looked like Don Quixote and Sancha Panza riding together up into the hills: AJ on the giant Gilbert and me on the small, fat grey. To enable me to keep up with Gilbert's long stride I had to keep Dobbin trotting, which was exhausting as he would far rather idle at a walk or jiggle sideways. Although the saddle fitted the cob it did not fit me, and I could feel a dreadful blister forming. By the time we reached the action, long after they had moved off from the meet, I was very uncomfortable.

The run took us down into the vale, and by dint of very hard work I kept Dobbin cantering. An opening presented a viable alternative to a thick hedge dividing two grass fields for most of the riders, each of whom in turn held open the five-barred gate for the one behind who would dextrously catch it with the bone handle of the hunting whip, and the gate was passed cleanly from whip to whip rather in the manner of a relay race. All was going well until my turn came; I caught the gate all right but reckoned without Dobbin, who stopped dead, and reversed a few paces making me release the gate, which swung to, trapping us firmly between it and the gatepost.

A rider behind pushed his whip handle against the gate with some force making it open, and riding through held it wide for us to continue. Dobbin stuck fast; he would go neither forward nor back, and it was not until someone hit him smartly across the rump with a whip that he gave a leap forward and we were away again. The blisters I earned that day from a saddle a size too small caused me to perch awkwardly on my three-legged stool at milking time for quite a few days, in spite of mother's ministrations with salt and water!

Dobbin's last act of disobedience before he got sent to a horse sale (he was far too well known in the district for a buyer to come forward) was to suddenly decide that he was not going to pass the convent, either between the shafts or under saddle. I don't know whether he had caught a glimpse of the black-robed figures and got scared, or whether it was just his bloody-mindedness and could have happened anywhere.

When Metford heard that we were having trouble, he volunteered to ride Dobbin and 'knock some sense into him'. He duly came up one afternoon as we started milking, and saddling Dobbin set off towards the convent. Nearly an hour later, purple in the face and sweating profusely, he was back: all that time he had been trying to get Dobbin past the convent but at last had to admit he was beaten. It was a sorry load for him to carry as he knew many would have seen his struggles with the recalcitrant grey, and would relate them with much embellishment in the public bars of the town.

AJ was renowned for his horse knowledge, and all sorts

of strange folk appeared to ask for solutions to various questions or to request help in healing the sick. Quite a few of the old countrymen mistrusted vets, a number could not have afforded the bills and some had been to the vet and still owed him and so could not go back. AJ was more than willing to oblige, and he carried recipes in his head for all manner of old potions and poultices handed down to him by his forefathers. He had kept a great many dogs over the years, once owning and breed-ing a number of Alsatians, which he doctored himself, and he gave me a recipe for mange potion with which I treated many dogs successfully over the years when this skin disease was rife.

We frequently had equine patients to stay, and one was a young mare who had kicked her trap to pieces when she was scared by a lorry while on a schooling drive down the main Taunton road. A sliver from the broken shaft had entered the knee joint at the back, and AJ diagnosed that the 'joint oil was running out'. He always said the best cure for cuts, bruises and any lacerations was cold running water, and for two hours every day, we took it in turns to stand and let water from the hose pipe trickle down the mare's leg. So used to this operation did she become that in a few days we were able to tie the pipe to her forearm, and she stood quite quietly while the soothing water ran over the injury. Whatever had been wrong with her, the cure worked, although it took several weeks, and the young mare went off home to continue her training.

Only once did I go on a day's hunting without AJ. He had long promised me a day out on Gilbert, and finally he kept his promise. I was to be escorted by an old friend of his, Mr Johnson, who had hunted the hills all his life and knew every inch of them.

The day of the hunt was gloriously sunny, and when the pack were laid on we set off down the hill, Mr Johnson on his short-tailed brown cob and me on the mighty Gilbert. Once on the flat with everyone galloping I was still trying to urge Gilbert out of his elastic and far-reaching trot into a more comfortable canter, but nothing doing. We sped along a valley and then climbed up into the hills, across the top, and suddenly were on the lip of one of the deep coombes. The riders started down, horses slipping and scrambling, and suddenly Gilbert slid a few feet. On stopping he shot me over his head and I rolled ignominiously down the slope to land in a gorse bush. The big horse stood still and solemnly watched my progress.

Gilbert's habit of not allowing the rider to mount from the ground was common knowledge, so one farmer stayed behind to give me a leg up. He was a rough chap with a hard face and bold eyes, and gave my leg a squeeze as he put me up, this accompanied by a stare that I found rather uncomfortable, but I thanked him politely and rode on to try to find Mr Johnson who was in the vanguard of the field. However, everyone seemed to have vanished and I endeavoured to locate them by listening for the sound of hounds and by following tracks.

The sides of the coombe blotted out sound, and there were so many marks of hoofs from previous hunts and those who rode the hills, that I was not sure which way to go. All I knew was that I wanted to get away from the farmer, so I put the big horse to a stiff climb and eventually found myself on high ground again. In vain I looked for a sight of riders or a sound of hounds. The bright sun was disappearing and a thick, cold mist rolling in from the sea, as can happen in that part of England. In less than no time the mist had enclosed me as if I were in a white paper bag. It was now intensely cold and damp, and I hesitated, not knowing quite what to do, when I heard the sound of hoofs and out of the mist rode the farmer I had tried to escape. He started talking in a jokey voice about the sudden mists that came down on the hills, and how they could hide anyone from sight. Then he began to tell me about the stallion he kept, and how excited his girl groom became when a mare came to be covered, and how she would put her hand in his breeches pocket. With that he lent over and squeezed my thigh, saying 'How about it then?'

It was time to rely on Gilbert's intelligence. I laid the reins on his neck, kicked him sharply and plunging into the fog left it to him. Ten minutes of Gilbert's racking trot and I heard the sound of hounds, and suddenly we were out of the mist and back in the sun, and there were riders and best of all Mr Johnson on his cob. I have never before or since been so glad to see friendly faces.

CHAPTER ELEVEN

At exactly noon one day in early summer we heard that there had been an outbreak of foot-and-mouth disease and an order had immediately been brought into force forbidding the movement of cloven-hoofed animals. At any other time of the year this would not have affected us, but in summertime we grazed the cows in the water meadows which lay across the road from the farm. In vain did AJ plead with the well-upholstered sergeant of police, who rode round the local farms on his shiny bicycle imparting the unwelcome news. If we could just bring the cows back. . . . The sergeant said 'No' in his firmest tones, and even AJ, with whom the officer was on the friendliest of drinking terms when off duty, could not bend him. The order said no movement of animals after noon, it was now after noon, and as far as the sergeant was concerned, no animals could be moved. This left the little matter of the milking.

AJ sat on the manger in the cowshed and thought. 'We shall 'ave to use Bob in thik pig cart,' he said after a pause. 'No good using that old devil of yours. We can take some churns, I'll have to get the dairy to leave extra, and buckets and stools, and if we can get 'em to stay still to span 'em, they should stand long enough to be milked.' It was a nice idea.

We drove Bob and his loaded cart down to the water meadows where our ladies were taking their ease in the bright green grass, resting after a morning's grazing, calmly and dreamily chewing the cud. We tied old Bob up under a willow tree. 'Leave 'em lay as long as possible,' AJ advised, unloading the cart quietly and neatly and handing me a stool, bucket and span. I put on my milking apron and cap so as to look as normal as possible and approached one of my charges. The sight of me so arrayed in the field, when she expected me to wear such apparel only in the shed, caused the cow to lurch to her feet in alarm, raise her tail high over her back and gallop off, spraying her displeasure behind her—it just missed me. Several of her companions followed suit. Old Granny, however, was still lying down. She regarded me with disdain from under the long lashes that fringed her lustrous dark eyes set in the creamy face, and batted flies off her cheeks with her ears. 'Up you get old girl,' I said conversationally, nudging her rump with my foot. Reluctantly she rose and stretched luxuriously, hollowing her back, peering round at me as I fastened the span on her hind legs. The span was a piece of hairy cord with a loop at one end and a wooden toggle at the other. It was passed round the offside leg, twisted into a figure of eight and then the toggle pushed through the loop once the cord had encircled the nearside leg. In theory it kept cows from kicking or, in this case, walking away.

Granny stood still, gazing into the middle distance. I

settled myself comfortably on my stool and began to milk. After a couple of minutes the novelty of staring into space and swishing flies off her back wore off, and Granny put her head down and began pulling at the grass. One pull, two pulls and she tried to walk forward for bite number three, but her hobbled back legs did not perform as they were wont to, and she threw up her head and kicked backwards, both legs at once, sending me and the bucket flying. AJ, who at that moment had persuaded Polly to allow him to sit under her, suffered the same fate, as that flighty lady took fright at old Granny's action. All, for a few moments, was chaos. I lost track of the time it took us to milk the cows that afternoon, but it was long after teatime when, drenched in sweat and manure, we drove Bob back to the farm with the small amount of milk the herd had allowed us to abstract. AJ deliberated as we strained and cooled the offering, and then announced he was going down to Jim for some stout rope. Jim was the ships' chandler and had a wonderful emporium on the little quay situated on the docks of the tidal river.

I finished off the work, and just as I was going to start for home, AJ drove up and stopped with a flourish. He had brought a large coil of rope. We would cut it into pieces and tie a length round each cow's horns; then when we went to milk, we could pick up a rope and have a cow ready. When we sat down we would anchor the cow by keeping a foot firmly on the rope. It sounded a good idea. The herd were not at all of that opinion.

The next morning we spent a precious hour catching cows and holding them still while we attached their ropes. One or two took fright and charged off, rope whipping round their heels and driving them on still faster. Polly, not having any horns, was furnished with a stirrup leather round the neck, to which her rope was attached. Once you had the rope you indeed had the cow. Spans were put in place, and we sat down and started to milk.Cows look stupid, but quite a lot goes on between the horns, and they soon learned that by taking dainty steps they could with difficulty walk forward while spanned, looking rather like Edwardian ladies in hobble skirts. This meant that they could go on feeding but they would suddenly take several steps forward to a better-looking patch, either leaving the milker sitting with a bucket between their knees and no cow, or else flat on their back as the rope whipped from under their feet.

The foot-and-mouth outbreak raged round the area for some weeks, fortunately not affecting stock on any of the land surrounding our acreage, but every farm was under restrictions in an attempt to try to arrest the spread of the outbreak. After a week or so the cows got quite used to the novel method of milking and would be waiting at the gate for us, and stood quite quietly while they were milked. Mercifully for much of the time it was fine weather, but we did strike a wet week when both AJ and I got drenched twice daily, sitting out as the rain poured down.

From my point of view there was only one major drawback to the arrangement, and that was Mr Phizaker-lea. He lived with his aged mother in a cottage on the lane leading to the water meadows. In his early thirties, he was

129

a cashier in the bank, always in a shiny blue suit and white shirt with slightly frayed cuffs. He was possibly the ugliest man I have ever seen, as his face had not one redeeming feature: the small nose with the bulbous end, always pink; the round, mild, apologetic, pale eyes with almost lashless lids; the thin mouth; and the pasty complexion, the whole topped by receding hair, made him anything but attractive. He was, however, a pleasant soul, and soon appeared at his gate to speak to me as I went back and forth early and late. One day when I passed he asked me to Sunday tea, saying his mother did not get out much, and that she had seen me pass and would like to know me. Silly me, I did not think anything of it. I should have noticed the red lights flashing; after all there had been Paul and 'Ceecil' to name but a few hopefuls.

However, one Sunday I spruced myself up and went to tea with the Phizakerleas. Mrs Phizakerlea was not all that old. She was a motherly type who obviously adored her one and only chick whom, it very soon turned out, she was anxious to see happily married. She talked endlessly about her son, while passing the sandwiches spread with their margarine ration and filled with home-grown tomatoes: how clever he was, how good he was to her and how fond of children. When she got out the photograph album depicting the baby, the schoolboy and the adolescent Mr P in all his unloveliness, the red lights really did begin to flash, and I made my escape as soon and as politely as possible.

All the time we had to milk in the meadows I had to run the gauntlet of Mr P or his smiling mother. I used up every excuse I could find to turn aside the many invitations, to tea, to supper, to the pictures: sorry I was working, going to a dog show, exercising the horses, etc. etc. At last the poor, desperate man got the message, or the foot-and-mouth ban was lifted, I cannot remember which. Anyway he ceased to pester me. I just hope that at sometime he found a girl to love him for his many attributes that I couldn't appreciate.

Once the restrictions were lifted life returned to normal and the cows to the shed for milking. AJ was suddenly struck down with a vicious flu bug. Like all big, hearty men who are seldom sick, when he finally went down with something he was really ill. The doctor told AJ's missus that her man was to be confined for at least two weeks in bed, as big chaps like him could easily develop pneumonia.

AJ's nephew Ray was not on leave, the odd-jobman Sam was unreliable and I could not hope to do all the work single-handed. AJ knew this and sent a message to the farm to tell me to contact the WLA lady and ask for a temporary girl. I telephoned, explained what had happened and she enthusiastically said she would send me a girl the next day.

Doreen arrived when I was halfway through milking. She was small and round with a pleasant smile and a lot of curly hair. Her uniform was complete and uncreased, and I guessed she had not been in the Land Army long. I was right. She had joined six weeks before and been sent to the local WLA hostel where she had had some training. It turned out that in civilian life she had been apprenticed to a dressmaker in London, but having seen the enticing recruitment posters depicting a shining-faced girl in immaculate breeches, with a gleaming pail on either arm, a Jersey cow in a manicured field and a whole panorama of trees and flowers behind, she had decided the country life was the one for her. She was not the only town girl to be taken in by this misleading poster.

Doreen could not milk; I showed her how, but every cow she sat under took umbrage and kicked. Eventually, I managed all 20 cows then in milk, and left Doreen cooling the milk and bottling in the dairy. This sounds a nice, easy operation, but actually required quite a lot of strength.

The cooler was of the waterfall variety and required an enormous amount of work to operate. This contraption had a pan on top, some five to six feet from the ground. The milk had to be lifted in pails and poured into the pan which had a brass tap. When the tap was opened the milk trickled down the undulating plates into the churn waiting below. Once the milk was cooled it had again to be tipped back into the pail and lifted into a similar pan on top of the bottler. This had a metal stand housing three bottles at a time, and three rubber nozzles enclosed in springs. Under the plate on which the bottles were placed were three metal handles; when these were pulled the nozzles came down into the bottles and this released the milk flow and the bottles filled. When filled, the bottles were taken off and arrayed in lines on the slate-topped table, and the cardboard tops pressed into place.

Once into the swing of things, cooling and bottling

was quite a pleasant operation, except in winter when your feet were frozen and your hands in danger of being frostbitten. The trouble was that Doreen was not very tall and certainly not strong: I had to keep going out to lift the milk, and only just avoided her letting water into the milk churn. I began to think I would have been better off without her.

A friend of AJ's had volunteered to come up and collect Bob and the float and do his round, and I took Doreen on my round. She was terrified of standing up in the float and spent much of the time on the move bent double. However, she was nice to the customers, and those who always revived me with refreshment managed to produce two cups of cocoa, although Doreen said she was not at all keen on the stuff. Arriving back with the empties a little later than usual we found that Sam was still there, and had not only lit the boiler but also cleaned out all the milking pails. Not having much faith in a woman's ability to manage without male help, he had obviously been inspired by the fact that he was now the only man about the place.

The next job was to wash the dirty milk bottles. I showed Doreen how to bale hot water into the first tank, the amount of powder to put in, and got her to fill the second tank with cold water. 'Now be careful,' I said quite sternly. 'The powder makes the water cloudy. Whatever you do, don't dive your hand in for a bottle. If one has broken you will get badly cut. Put your hand in flat and carefully. It takes a bit longer but it is well worth it.' 'Right ho,' smiled the girl, and dived her hand downwards into the hot water.

There was blood everywhere. Sam suggested binding the wound up with cobwebs—an old-fashioned remedy to stop bleeding—but the broken bottle had cut quite deeply between thumb and forefinger. So I tied a tourniquet made with a dairy cloth round Doreen's wrist, bundled her into the float and clattered down to the casualty department of the local hospital—and that was the last I saw of Doreen.

Next day I got Clara, a sour, straw-haired girl with weak eyes and a sniff. She could just about milk, did not like horses, and performed all her functions grudgingly, but she was better than nothing and stayed until AJ was back at work.

Not being a great one for authority, I kept a low profile and hoped the lady from the WLA would leave me alone. However one day I received an invitation: she was giving tea to all the Land Girls in her area one Sunday and hoped I would attend. My mother said I ought to go, so reluctantly I agreed. What to wear? 'Well,' said my mother, 'no one goes out to tea on Sunday in uniform. You had better wear your suit.' It was a cool autumn so I arrayed myself in the blue and white dog's-tooth check garment kept for special occasions, a reasonable pair of shoes, white blouse and a pull-on hat. Out of a company that seemed to be about a hundred, I was the only girl not in uniform. It was a deeply embarrassing experience. All eyes seemed to be turned on me: I stood out like a wilting bluebell in a turnip field. Many of the girls knew one another, as they worked in gangs on arable farms or in forestry. I knew no one and, come to that, had no desire to.

Tea was set out in buffet fashion in the big dining room of a beautiful old house, and I was longing to know how the hostess had procured so much food given that rationing was tight. Before the repast was served our hostess gave us a 'jolly hockeysticks' talk about what a good job we were all doing, and how healthy and happy we all looked, and how we were to bring any problems to her at any time. I know she meant well. I collected a plateful of food, tucked myself into a corner and consumed it, and as soon as possible sneaked out to my bicycle and rode home vowing never to accept another invitation from the WLA, whatever mother advised, and I never did—not that they did not come, oh no.

Every so often I was bidden to take part in one of the parades organised to march through the town on a Sunday, by the Wings for Victory or the Spitfire Fund. My instructions told me to attend at such and such a place at a certain time, and to wear full uniform and carry a hay rake, pitchfork or some other tool of the trade. Mother and I would sit up in the window of our bedroom and watch the parade: 12 soldiers, 12 sailors, 12 airmen, 12 nurses, 12 wardens, 12 fire-watchers, 12 Home Guard and so on, but only ever 11 Land Girls. Just to pay the organisers back for the lost 18 months' service and that ghastly tea party, I never wrote to say I was not coming.

On a Sunday I usually went riding after washing the milk bottles when I was not saving up half days in order to make a full Saturday and go off to a dog show. We started earlier on Sunday because the milk lorry came an hour before the usual time, and anyway AJ liked to have a good two hours or so for lunchtime drinking. On the Sabbath we only did the necessary things like feeding, cleaning out, and the milking and delivery and washing the few bottles that were put out—somehow people never left out their full complement of bottles on a Saturday night. This meant I was through work by 11:30, so Gilbert and I went off for a nice ride.

AJ changed his habits on Sunday, not making for Metford's hostelry but for one up the hill from where he lived, a rather larger place called the Halfway House. One Sunday I had ridden up into the hills and came back down this road and on passing the pub was hailed by the locals sitting outside in the sun, and inside through the wide open doors. 'Come in and have a drink!' shouted one—so I did, riding Gilbert straight into the bar. It caused quite a sensation as the big horse simply filled the place, but everyone had a good laugh, Gilbert was given an apple by the landlady and AJ, not generous when it came to money, actually bought me a lemonade for my cheek. It was a story told around for quite some time. If either of us was driving Bob and stopped at a pub for any reason, those within the bar who knew the old cob always brought him out some beer in a glass. Bob would fasten his long top lip over the rim and allowed the liquor to trickle down his throat as he raised his head, sighing deeply afterwards and licking his lips with pleasure. It was his little party piece and he enjoyed the applause that inevitably followed from any bystanders.

The grains for the cows were fetched on three afternoons a week; on the other two I had to collect the swill for the pigs from the Royal Engineers cookhouse. The regiment had been billeted in the town for some time and was glad to have its wastage taken away and used to good purpose. The sergeant cook was a Scotsman, inevitably called Jock, a square, jolly man who made wonderful currant cake in great flat trays. When I called there was always a chunk for me and a mug of good, strong army tea.

The boys in the cookhouse were a nice bunch, treating me like a sister and proud to show me photographs of their families and tell me their plans for when the war was over. At Christmas we took them holly and mistletoe to decorate the cookhouse, and AJ provided some home-made cider for the celebrations, and even slipped Jock a pound as a 'thank you' for the swill. Of course all the boys kissed me under the mistletoe, and the fruitcake was replaced with mince-pies. It was with real regret that we heard the regiment was moving out, and we had some sorrowful goodbyes when AJ and I went with small gifts for the boys with whom we had become firm friends.

For a month no other regiment came in and we were wondering what to do about swill, when AJ appeared one day to inform me that he had got the offcuts from the fishmonger. He left two high-smelling bins at the farm and took two more home. We only had two sties at the farm and fed around six to eight pigs, and unlike Mrs AJ we did not have a boiler to cook the swill, so it was fed raw. It was quite warm when the fish swill arrived: the smell was so awful that when I used it I tied a scarf round my nose, but the pigs found the new food much to their taste. On the third day when I took the lid off the second bin, it was to find one heaving mass of maggots. This was too much. I told AJ that if he wanted to use fish swill he could in future feed the pigs himself, at which he roared with laughter and said he did not think I minded anything, so I briskly retorted that I did—snakes and maggots being two of them. However, the maggots, or 'gentles' as AJ called them, were not to be fed to the pigs until he had been to see the local schoolmaster who was a keen fisherman. This gentleman, on hearing the glad news, quickly arrived at the farm and the two of them bent their heads over the stinking bin, picking out by hand the largest and fattest 'gentles' for bait.

The American Army arrived unexpectedly. We had heard vaguely that they might be billeted on the town but thought it just a rumour. One day they were not there and the next they were. The town was never to be the same again. Many of the soldiers moved into the old RE buildings and took over the cookhouse, and a large number were billeted in tents put up on the old fairfield which lay on one side of the road up which I had to drive back and forth to the farm. The Yanks, who were immaculately dressed and very well paid, soon had many of the females in the town in thrall. This gave them the idea that all females were fair game. I was whistled at and propositioned as I drove along. Once a soldier stepped out and grabbed Shaddock's bridle and called out 'Give us kiss Babe.' My trusty steed came to my rescue as she made a grab for the man's arm, sinking her big yellow teeth into his smart uniform and sending him reeling back with a shout of pain. The Americans took readily to the local brew of rough cider but did not quite understand its potency and would get very drunk. On these occasions one of their favourite and less pleasant tricks as they rolled back to the fairfield was to fill all the empty milk bottles put out on doorsteps with urine!

Although AJ soon had a contract for all the swill from the American cookhouse, I only went twice to collect it. The sight of a girl with a pony and cart coming to collect bins of waste was something strange to the Americans. Perhaps in their country the people who collected waste food were considered 'poor white trash' and not fit to associate with ordinary mortals. Anyway, whatever the reason, they were so rude and offensive to me that I asked to be relieved of the duty, and after that AJ did the collection. The pigs had never had it so good: from the meagre wastage of peelings and crusts from the RE they suddenly found themselves dining on whole chickens, turkey, lumps of ham, cakes, whole puddings, biscuits, butter and once AJ had to make a special collection of a cartful of loaves. When food was in such short supply it seemed wicked that so much was wasted. AJ quickly got to know the Americans who mattered, and in less than no time was receiving a steady supply of tinned goods of all sorts which he was able to use for barter at the highest level!

CHAPTER TWELVE

When I first went to work for AJ, Billy the Bull was in residence. He was a huge Shorthorn of advanced years, and spent his life chained by the neck in a small wooden barn at the end of the cowshed, and seemed only to come out when one of the cows needed serving, a mission that was always accomplished while I was on my round, AJ and Sam attending to this. Perhaps it was years of boredom culminating in complete frustration that caused Billy to go beserk, but one morning when we were just finishing the milking there was a great roar from the barn, and a tremendous crash of splintering timbers that shook the whole building. Abandoning buckets and stools we both rushed out in time to see Billy, who had wrenched his great chain free from the wall and had it dangling round his neck, breast the rails round the yard and snap them like matchsticks, before charging off down the field uttering bellows loud enough to wake the dead.

AJ dispatched me on my bike to a local farming friend, and I was to enlist all the help I could, for Billy had to be recaptured before he broke out of our fields and on to the road. In 20 minutes there were some six assorted men and boys in the yard, some armed with pitchforks, and they advanced down the field with the idea of driving Billy into the other, smaller yard at the rear of the sheds. Billy was pawing the ground with his giant hoofs and uttering great cries of rage, and every now and then advanced on the hedge that divided two of our fields, and uprooted a part of it on his huge, spreading horns. At the sight of the small flotilla advancing towards him, Billy prepared for battle, and the little flock fled back, pitchforks and all, to the doubtful shelter of the cowshed. Several similar sorties met with the same fate. Billy was getting wilder and wilder. He once galloped right up to the shed where we were all cowering and peered in at the window, and it was possible to see the glaring red-rimmed eyes, and the saliva trickling from his mouth.

The considered opinion of all was that the bull had gone mad and the vet would have to be sent for. The vet was one of the old sort, in his early seventies, tall and handsome with a wide sweep of white moustache; he wore immaculate breeches and boots and a grey bowler hat, and was far more likely to be out hunting than in the surgery. I was again dispatched on my bicycle, this time to a nearby house known to have a telephone, to ring the vet, and ask him to come and dispatch Billy. The old man was actually in the surgery, but when he heard my request flatly refused to come near the farm saying he had no intention of tackling a mad bull at his time of life, and offered to ring the knackerman as he was the one to deal with such a situation. I returned to report the news.

By now Billy had worked himself into a greater fury, and was thundering about the field bellowing and tossing lumps of turf and bushes about like cotton wool. Our little army melted away, and when Billy had gone to the far end of the field, AJ and I made a dash for the dairy and together hurriedly bottled up, and I went off on my round.

When I got back the place was deserted. There were the tracks where a big lorry had backed in—and Billy had departed. AJ came in the afternoon and I asked what happened. 'Oh they got their ways,' he said. 'Didn't take no time at all, shame, he was a good bull.'

The badly damaged barn had to be rebuilt and this proved a good excuse to make it into a stable, a far more satisfactory proposition, while the yard fence was reconstructed by lengths of metal piping that arrived from some unknown source.

For over a year we were without a bull. When the cows needed serving AJ would put a halter on them and lead them off to a Shorthorn owned by a local farming friend. One spring day he came in for afternoon milking and announced that he had bought a youngster that would arrive at about teatime. I thought he meant a heifer, so I was not very enthusiastic when his purchase turned out to be an 18 month old Devonshire bull. This handsome red fellow owned a rapidly expanding pair of horns that stuck out each side of his head. He was quite peaceful and was put out to graze in the small paddock. The dry cows and a couple of heifers were turned away in a field some mile distant, and it was with no little alarm that I received the order from AJ to lead the new arrival up to the field and turn him out there. I asked why he could not do it, but he said gruffly that he had 'something else on.'

Billy the Second was not all that tall, but he was very bulky. I did not relish moving him, but obediently drove him into the shed and, as he did not yet have a ring in his nose, put a halter on him. We got on to the road quite easily, but once there the youngster began to look around in an interested fashion. I had to keep my hand fairly close to his head, for if I had tried to lead him on a long rope and he had started off I could not have held him. However, the problem was whether to walk so that his left horn was behind my body or in front. I tried walking slightly ahead but when his attention was attracted and he turned his head to the right the horn dug me in the back. Then when I tried walking slightly behind him, and he swung his head to the left, I got the horn in my solar plexus. Of course we had to meet all kinds of people I knew, full of jokey remarks like, 'Why don't you get on his back?' and 'Ride 'im, cowboy.'

The small amount of traffic usually encountered on the road seemed to have increased that day. Several dispatch riders passed at speed and Billy the Second and I finished up in various front gardens. I was nearly at the field when an army convoy approached: I knew I could never hold on, so I started to run and Billy the Second thought this was entrancing and leapt in the air making infantile noises as he did so, and it was only by good luck that we reached the lane to the field before the big vehicles thundered past. I was so exhausted by the time I had lugged open the gate that I failed to remember that it was a bull with horns and not a horse with just ears that I was loosing. The halter failed to come over the horns and before I knew it Billy the Second was away, prancing and kicking, the three cows and two heifers joining in with wild abandon, while hanging from his horns was AJ's best horse halter. By then I had ceased to care and trudged back to the farm and, when he arrived, I told AJ that if he wanted his halter he could go and get it himself—he gave a grin and said nothing.

With no arable land to cultivate our only tasks other than the dairy side of things were hedge trimming, ditching and chain-harrowing. We rented several extra fields which we also harrowed, but did not have to do anything to the water meadows which the cows grazed from mid-May through the summer. Our own fields and two we rented were shut up for hay by the end of April, and were first chain-harrowed to break up all the cowpats and horse droppings. It was a peaceful occupation, well away from the road, with wild flowers blooming in the hedges and the tall trees shading the edges of the field. There were all kinds of birds then, and when I stopped for a rest it was to hear the skylark high above and the scolding of the blackbirds as I disturbed them in their flight back and forth to feed their young. Not all days were fine, some were very cold and the walking up and down kept me warm, and some were wet and very unpleasant. I used the horses in turn, but preferred Shaddock, as she had the best stride and I could get over the field quicker, although she was not as reliable as the other two, who did not suddenly take off as the old mare would on occasions.

Haymaking was a busy time. We got to the farm and milked earlier, and I was back from the round and washed up in time to do my stint with the pitchfork, the swathe turner or horse rake. A couple of old boys who had retired from farming came and did a bit during the day, and when his dustman's duties were ended, Mr Bowden appeared and worked hard enough for two men. If Ray was at home he lent a hand, and old Sam rambled down so as not to miss anything. Other characters came for an hour or so, mostly I think to partake of the refreshment. Each morning AJ would bring four large stone jars of cider to the field, and deposit one and a tin mug in each of the four hedges. When the workers got thirsty they stopped and helped themselves. I had a couple of bottles of some kind of fruit drink, whatever was on offer at the time, and one year Mrs AJ produced a bottle of lime juice which gave me terrible colic.

The swathe turner was easy to use and simply did what it said: turned over the newly mown swathes of grass to the sun and air. The horse rake was purgatory. The operator perched up on an iron seat behind the horse, while the huge semi-circular tines of the rake were situated behind. A large lever dropped the tines to the ground and as the horse moved forward the hay was gathered up. The idea was to leave the gathered hay in neat rows to be put up by hand in 'pucks' or haycocks ready for collection. When the rake reached the line of gathered hay, the operator was supposed to raise the tines and let the gathered hay fall into the row. However, our horse rake was of great antiquity and very rusty, and no amount of oil caused it to operate easily. I had to use two hands and exert all my strength to get the lever up or down, and this meant holding the reins between my knees and just hoping that Shaddock would not take off at the crucial moment. It was exhausting work and none of my hay rows were ever very straight or tidy.

It was still the practice then, on small farms, for the hay to be tossed about by someone wielding a pitchfork, or two-tined prong as it was often called. I did my stint at tossing hay, which artists portray as such a romantic occupation; actually it is really hard work, and a few hours at this caper in the full sun can leave one drenched with perspiration and totally exhausted.

We worked every evening at building the ricks. One was made down in the field and another couple in our small rickyard up at the farm. The hay was carted in the afternoon and evening, which meant we were joined by a small number of bright-faced children, including Young Bowden who was quite useful but had to be kept away from the cider. The children enjoyed riding on the hay loads up to the farm and reminded me of my happy times when I had been their age not so long before.

The building of the ricks was a meticulous affair. First we put down the 'steddle', a deep layer of dry sticks and branches exactly the shape and size for the rick. This was to allow air to circulate through the rick, as hay heats easily and ricks have been known to go up in flames. The first load was tossed haphazard on to the steddle, and then the rick-maker took over, working from the outside of the rick inwards, and then filling the middle. After the second load the feeder joined in: this is the person who takes the hay as it is pitched up and feeds it to the rick-maker, and this was my job. We had an ancient elevator which was propped against the rick once it got too high for the men to chuck the forkfuls of hay up to the feeder: then the hay was put on the elevator, which was run by a very smelly engine, and slowly it chugged its way to the top.

In quiet weather the whole process worked like clockwork but in a gale it was very hard labour, especially if we were pitching into the wind. Three men were needed for loading a cart—we only used the pig cart and a borrowed light, flat-bed wagon—and two for tossing the hay up to the rick-maker or loading the elevator. The children and any mothers who had come down were given wooden rakes to scrape up hay that had escaped the horse rake or loaders: hay was a valuable commodity and waste in wartime not encouraged.

By dusk the children had gone home, and Mrs AJ would have arrived wearing her wide-brimmed, navy-blue straw-hat, anchored by a vast silver-knobbed hatpin, and her spotless white pinafore, riding her upright bicycle with the large basket on the front and the box on the carrier. In her box she brought lumps of fat, boiled bacon, a pound or two of cheese (extra rations of cheese were allocated for farmworkers), a loaf or two of bread, pickled onions, hard-boiled eggs and sometimes a fruit cake. We all sat down round the rick leaning back on its fragrant bulk, eating and drinking, laughing and telling yarns, while the bats swept overhead and the mosquitoes sang as they feasted on our bare arms. Food consumed, the men lit their pipes and finished the last of the cider, and then wearily, and, in some cases, a little unsteadily, we all made our way home.

Once the ricks were up they needed protection from the elements, and Old Sam was a dab hand at thatching them against the weather. In spite of his age and rheumatism he could get up the ladder with surprising agility, and work all day with never a complaint. Once the ricks were thatched we could relax a little. Come the winter, however, and the ricks assumed an important focal point in the life of the farm, for every day huge slices had to be cut out to feed the stock. This was accomplished by the use of a giant knife blade mounted on a strong steel shaft and finished with a horizontal wooden handle. One stood over the blade as it were, and plunged it up and down, and mind where you had your feet.

When the rick was first opened only AJ, or Ray if he were on leave, ever went up and cut hay, but by the time the rick was reduced by half it was my turn to cut the fragrant slabs which the cows consumed with relish to the last slice. I cannot say I was much good with the knife: it required quite a deal of strength and although in those days I was no weakling, I often got the knife stuck and could not get it to budge either up or down. I felt such an idiot having to shout for help, which always came accompanied by a broad grin from whoever answered the plaintive cries.

Winter was hard work as we had to use both chaff and root cutters, neither of them exactly a rest cure. Chaff was produced by putting hay or oat straw through the machine which was turned by hand, and was not a bad job, but the root cutter was jolly hard work. It was a large cast-iron apparatus on legs. Inside, a large roller with teeth

148

was attached to an iron handle. The roots were tipped in and the operator turned the handle—and if this sounds easy, believe you me, it was not, particularly when the roots were solid in frosty weather. Each winter AJ used to say 'mind your fingers', and proceed to tell the gruesome story of a man who was pushing the roots down in the machine and forgot to stop turning the handle and how his hand was all mashed up.

AJ bought in loads of roots, mangolds or swedes, or acquired a load by some kind of barter. The chopped roots were added to the grains and any meal or cake we could purchase. Animal feed was rationed during the war, and there was much wheeling and dealing to get a little extra in country districts. Once we had some great sheets of cake, like partitions to a shed, and had quite a time breaking them up into manageable pieces. This was called 'decorticated cattle-cake'. It smelt terrible and heaven only knows what it contained. We did not ask questions in wartime, being only too glad to get any kind of animal feed. For a week the cows resolutely refused to touch the new food, snorting loudly at it and goggling their eyes. However, after a time some hardy soul must have tasted it and passed it as safe for bovine consumption, because they all suddenly decided it was delicious. Oats for the horses were in short supply, but every so often at dusk, a wagon loaded with straw would turn into our farm. As we had no arable land we had to purchase straw and so the load did not attract attention. By the time it was off-loaded and stacked it would be dark, and no one could see us carrying away the sacks of oats that were lying in the bottom of the wagon!

We were also keen to get extra food for ourselves, whenever possible. Once milk was rationed an extra bottle to the grocer could produce a pot of jam, some margarine or butter, while the pork butcher could often find the odd half pound of sausages when his wife fancied a milk-pudding. The sweet shop would have a great long queue waiting outside when people knew a delivery was due, all anxious to be able to spend their coupons, but a little something was always under the counter for an extra bottle of milk. AJ used to let me have the occasional half-dozen eggs, but most of his surplus was earmarked for bargaining.

The rationing of milk made things very difficult on the round. Unless people had close relatives serving in the forces, the war was just a bit of an inconvenience, and any more rationing done only to annoy everyone! When rationing came in we left little notes to tell people how much milk they would be entitled to. I had one customer who particularly resented this. She had always been one of the worst at paying her milk bill and was always out when the money was due; at least she never answered the door, but I saw the lace curtain twitch on more than one occasion. AJ had taken to dropping in on her unexpectedly on his way home, and every now and then had abstracted a few shillings from her.

She was waiting for me the day after receiving her note and flew out in a rage, flourishing a feather-duster, her hair tied up in a turban, and I burst out laughing, thinking she must be imitating some stage character. But she was deadly serious and tore into me for leaving an insulting note just because she was a poor woman with no husband or children to stand up for her and just because she could not always meet her bills on time but she always paid, and on and on without a pause for breath. I could not get a word in edgeways, and retreated to my float and drove away to leave her still shouting. Every day she left a note saying 'Two pints', and every day I left her her statutory pint, and then she took to opening her upstairs window and shouting at me. When AJ received the same treatment he stopped serving her and let the Co-op take her over. I am not sure if they managed to get through to her. I hope they enjoyed the task.

When the end of the war was in sight two things occurred which heralded the end of my time at the farm and, indeed, in the Land Army: AJ's nephew Ray got demobbed and his niece, who I had replaced, called at the farm and asked if she could come back and work for him. AJ was a kindly man and although he never gave praise I was aware that he had valued all the hard work I had put in over my three years on the farm. It was with a red face and downcast eye that he started mumbling something about the family, so I saved him embarrassment and said I quite understood that he would want to employ his kith and kin again, and he was pathetically grateful to be relieved of the job of sacking me or making me redundant after so long. It was in a way sad to say goodbye to the old farm; but I too had to start a new life once the hostilities were at an end.

Some eight years later I went back. AJ's daughter had met someone who knew me and who had given her my

address, and out of the blue I received a letter from her
inviting me down to see the farm to which her parents
had moved and where she and her husband and little son
were also living. By then I was also married and had a
small daughter, and I was keen to show my husband
where I had spent the war.

Eight years is a long time. The town was expanding
and many of the old buildings, such as the terrace where
the old folk had lived, had been knocked down and ugly
modern bungalows put in their place. AJ had bought a
small farm about a mile beyond the old farm, which was
no more. A huge housing estate sprawled where once
there had been green fields, and I was told it was owned
by the Co-op, possibly paying AJ out for landing them
with the customer who never paid her bills!

As we drove into the new farm I could see how things
were changing. In the old days the family had boasted
nothing more in the way of transport than the horses and
bicycles: now a smart car was under one shed, a motorised
milk float under the other. The family came out smiling
to greet us, AJ a little older and heavier, Mrs AJ with her
kind face, her hair now greying, and AJ's daughter with
her husband who ran the farm and made the decisions. I
was shown the spanking new milking parlour and the
electric milking machine, a clean dairy and a bottling
shed. There were still a few horses about, but AJ had had
a heart attack and did not ride so much. Gilbert had badly
injured a leg out hunting and been put down at his stable
door, and AJ had paid a contractor to come and dig a big
hole in the orchard so the old horse could sleep at home.

It was the only time I ever saw AJ at all sentimental, and I could swear his eyes were moist when he told me the story. For old times' sake I rode one of the horses out and around the old haunts, but it was not the same. They say you should never go back.

Perhaps it would be as well if I also kept out of farming museums, just in case they decide to put me on show in the 'Extinct Species' section!

My work with animals and my time on the land not only fulfilled my wish to work on a farm as Buttercup Jill. They also gave me many skills that were to be of enormous use in later years. I married an aspiring actor, fresh from six years in the Army, not a farmer as expected. Although my husband had farming relatives, strangely enough in Gloucestershire, where he had spent happy childhood holidays, he had never thought of being a farmer. A few years of marriage to me, however, and he found himself getting handy with the hoe, the milking bucket and the hay rake during times when he was 'resting'. At the end of eight years he gave up the stage and found full-time work on a farm. Together we had many farming adventures, but that, of course, is another story!

Farming Press Books & Videos

BOOKS

One Dog, His Man & His Trials   **Marjorie Quarton**

Shep's tales of a sheepdog's life in Ireland with its rogues, adventures and humorous encounters, canine and human.

The Hired Lad   **Ian Thomson**

A young man's first work on a Scottish farm when horses were yielding to tractor and bothy life was rough and ready.

On the Smell of an Oily Rag   **John Cherrington**

The classic account of a farming life including early days in New Zealand and Patagonia.

VIDEOS

Harnessed to the Plough   **Roger & Cheryl Clark with Paul Heiney**

Roger and Cheryl Clark demonstrate a year of contemporary horse-drawn cultivations and harvesting on their Suffolk farm. Additional commentary by Paul Heiney.

For more information or for a free illustrated catalogue of all our publications please contact:

**Farming Press Books & Videos,
Wharfedale Road, Ipswich IP1 4LG, United Kingdom**
Telephone **(0473) 241122**   *Fax* **(0473) 240501**

Farming Press Books & Videos is part of the Morgan-Grampian Farming Press Group which publishes a range of farming magazines: *Arable Farming, Dairy Farmer, Farming News, Pig Farming, What's New in Farming.* For a specimen copy of any of these please contact the address above.